Principles of Cartel Disruption:

Accelerate and Maximize Performance

BY DAVID RADLO

Interior book layout and design: Justin Oefelein of SPX Multimedia

Printed in the United States of America

Dedication:

This book is dedicated to Ben and Jess, who put up with Dad's coaching and cooking growing up. I love you both very much.

Author's Note:

Right before publishing, America lost a great hero. I wanted to recognize the memory of WWII War Veteran, Coach Bill Tighe who I played for and coached with at Lexington High School in Lexington, MA. For 52 years and 514 games, Coach Tighe was the longest serving successful head high school football coach ever in America. He passed away at the age of 95 in 2020 due to Covid-19 complications. Coach Tighe achieved his mission many times over in training young adults how to win at football, family, and life.

Table of Contents

SECTION 1 - MARKET RESEARCH AND VALUE PROPOSITION

SECTION 2 - FUNDING

SECTION 3 - OPERATIONAL EXCELLENCE

SECTION 4 - GIVING BACK

Foreword

For most, disruption isn't easy, but it sure is fun, especially when it works. You have to break eggs to make an omelet, someone was heard to say. I am at my best disrupting because for me it came naturally. Upon my arrival at NFL Properties in 1979, I found a woefully undermarketed, hidebound, and conservative entity in the NFL, which had laser focus on the game on the field but little appreciation for what a fan like myself actually wanted to enhance their experience in consuming NFL football. We changed that with innovation, not always well received, by offering rabid fans much more than flame-retardant T-shirts bought at Sears or electric football games. We made available actual game wear, equipment, and apparel worn by the coaches and players on gameday. We issued team-identified credit cards and dressed golfer Payne Stewart in NFL-identified golf wear he wore winning two major tournaments. It all worked. Money was made as fans happily paid to wear what the pros wear. We also generated major sponsorships beyond Punt, Pass and Kick with tie-ins with Canon, Coke, GTE, and Apple, among others, with plausible official designations and with food companies that participated in a fun, food, and football-themed tailgate promotion. We also disrupted the cartel by forcing Topps, a one-time cartel in the football trading card business, to work with the league in its product offerings. The NFL business exploded. What was once viewed as crass commercialization is now the norm at the NFL.

After leaving NFL Properties, I thought I was every bit the entrepreneur that the NFL owners were and, more realistically, that NFL licensees of jackets, hats, trading cards, and other marketed items were. At the time, brands like Clearly Canadian, Snapple, and Arizona were disrupting the beverage business, earning them fortunes on buyouts from big players like Pepsi and Coke. With a partner, I jumped in with a brand called SoBe, a line of nutritionally enhanced juices and teas, and in the process created the now much-copied nutraceutical functional category. We added vitamins, minerals, and herbs to great-tasting drinks that promised to make the drinker smarter, skinnier, and sexier, with names like Power, Wisdom, and Energy. SoBe wasn't really much more than sugar water. It also had a fun-filled fourth dimension in the trademark lizard and the slogan "Drain the Lizard." I took a significant risk, betting the family house to fund the concept. With tenacity, hard work, and a little luck, it worked. SoBe sold to PepsiCo after five years for $370 million. Disruption can be rewarding. Disrupting a cartel like the beverage biz can be especially rewarding.

Dave Radlo can help you wring significant value out of disrupting a cartel. A cartel is an association of manufacturers or suppliers with the purpose of maintaining prices at a high level and restricting competition. Dave has significant success and experience with cartel disruption and he is sharing it with readers through his great book *The Principles of Cartel Disruption.*

I have known Dave Radlo for several years through our mutual support of Tufts University's Innovation and athletic programs. We share our love for giving back to Tufts University and its students. We are also in agreement that there are key principles required to disrupt a cartel. In this book, Dave shares many of the principles and hidden secrets for cartel disruption.

Dave, along with his partners, developed what is now a multibillion dollar category of specialty eggs (those are the proverbial eggs we broke earlier). He developed consumer food brands and line extensions such as Egg-Land's Best Cage Free, Born Free, and various private label lines. The brand creation showed impressive growth and results. Further, the creation of commercial Cage Free, other humane initiatives, and Commercial Free Range is notable. Equally impressive is the use of technology and biotechnology as a differentiator and competitive advantage.

Dave was part of the Vicam start-up, which provided for safer food through pathogen testing. Technology also drove the start-up of Born Free Eggs, with a focus on food safety and packaging from new technology.

Currently, Dave is a partner and board member of Canadian Next Remedies, which is a technology-driven company with revolutionary PTS biotechnology. The products are highly bioavailable, nano-versions of fat-soluble vitamins and supplements, making it possible for them to be carried through the bloodstream and reach their destinations in a fraction of the time the full digestive process would take and with more efficacy, which means the stuff actually works. Dave has also worked to raise additional capital, as well as on roll-up strategies with Venture Capital and Private Equity Firms to effectively accelerate growth.

Meanwhile, Dave has brought novel, battle-tested methods of entrepreneurial innovation and acceleration to universities, where students and faculty have transformed learning these principles into effective disruption and acceleration, as well as financial and commercial success.

Dave is an innovative and creative entrepreneur, and it's fun to work with him. *The Principles of Cartel Disruption* is a must-read for anyone that wants to improve their results and perhaps disrupt a cartel while doing so!

John Bello
Chairman, Reed's, Inc. (NASDAQ: REED)
Founder and Former CEO of South Beach Beverage Co. (SoBe Nutritional Beverages)
Former President, NFL Properties, the Commercial and Licensing Arm of the NFL

Introduction

For many years, people have said to me, "David, you need to write a book." So, for those that have challenged me, here it is. In summary, I have written this book to provide you with lessons on your road to success. I am a cartel disrupter and accelerator.

This book characterizes in clarity the secrets of disruption and acceleration. In various aspects of my life, I have learned and practiced these principles of disruption. I was able to crack a multibillion-dollar egg cartel and grew my company by more than a 30X growth alignment value with successful customer-focused strategic innovation, leadership, and process excellence and with sustainable and purposeful service to the community and service to this great nation.

Oxford Dictionary defines a cartel as *an association of manufacturers or suppliers with the purpose of maintaining high prices and restricting competition*. That sums up many closely held industries, organizations, and, at times, individual countries or geographic areas.

Innovation is the process where one introduces a new method, idea, product, or service that brings change and new ideas to the market.

To be successful at innovative disruption and various elements of business, nonprofits, law, medicine, research, and in many disciplines, you must be able to deal effectively with relationships and with pain points, or as my former head of production, Tom Shea, used to say, "opportunities." The way I see it, the bigger the pain point, the bigger the opportunity for success and the more valuable you become to your customers and your organization.

I am a disrupter and an innovator. My success as a strategic innovator has come by maximizing value through aligning people, process, strategy, and sustainability. To become a disrupter and innovator, it will be your job to break the rules. And yes, at times you will irritate people that are resistant to change. Often it is the power structure in an industry that resists.

The hallmark of my disruption and innovation success was partnering with and developing the footprint that de-commoditized a multibillion-dollar egg cartel. This was made possible through the successful development of value-added products. I will take you through that journey in the pages of this book and how new products and brands can be developed, incubated, and accelerated.

MARKET RESEARCH AND VALUE PROPOSITION

CHAPTER ONE

PRINCIPLE I: Understand Your Opportunity and Create a Winning Value Proposition

I was sitting by the banks of Walden Pond, which overlooks where Henry David Thoreau once lived in his shelter. As I peered down at the book I was reading by Tom Peters, a well-known author of business management practices, there it was: "Make a new pie," with an excellent value proposition. This line created a spark for me. The way to be successful was not to attack other people's markets and gain share through price. To create a new pie, you have to find a new category. By having a small, fast-growing niche within a large industry, you can dominate. That's where you can create your pie. Steve Jobs did this with Apple.

Later that day, I had lunch at Helen's in Concord, Massachusetts, with Ken Lizzotte. Ken was the head of the Boston CEO's Club and head of conservation efforts at Thoreau's birthplace. I continued to discuss and ponder Tom Peter's statement about making a new pie. According to Ken, Henry David Thoreau invented the graphite pencil. He created a new pie. Perhaps Thoreau dreamed up the graphite pencil while sitting at Walden Pond.

As you will see in this chapter, I began to look for opportunities to add value to the egg industry. Everyone had branded products. I began to think about what the current economic, social, and technological trends were. How could a new pie be created?

First, we considered the packaging. It was drab. What could be done to improve it? Was there anything that could be done technologically? Could a stamp or etching be placed on an egg? What could be done to meet social needs for animal rights and nutrition? This process is how my partners and team and I created our pie. We created a specialty category that started as a segment of the broader category. It has grown into its category now. That day, I added to Tom Peter's analysis; one should target a small segment of a broad category filled with fast-growing trends.

Identify Your Customers' Needs

If you want to understand your customers, market research is required. You gain a competitive edge when you know your customers well. To create an effective strategy, you must identify the buying patterns, demographics, market trends, and pain points that affect them. When your customers' purchasing behavior matches your marketing plan, you are on the road to success. That's why market research is so important.

There are many ways to collect data about your customers. You can use customer interviews, multiple-choice surveys, and focus groups. I have had success with the use of focus groups. I've also hired market research professionals to gather data. If you don't have the funding and have to bootstrap this part of the process, you can survey twenty-five separate customers using open-ended, closed-end, and strategic questioning. The key is not to ask leading questions, so your data isn't skewed.

During the market research process, you will test your potential ideas. You want to find out what your customer is thinking and how desirable they feel your product is to them. The goal is to find out what types of propositions are desirable. After that, you can test concept elements. The information you collect from the research will allow you to see if there is an opportunity for new technology, growing or shrinking markets, and market disruption. When you understand the customer, you can develop a good, better, and best principle of products so that expansion can happen from there.

Test the packaging for your product. For some products, the packaging may be important, but for others, it may not. For example, recycled packaging may be an essential characteristic to your customers if they care about sustainability. The key is to create a product and packaging that meets your customers' satisfaction.

I'm going to walk you through the market research process with a case study. I will share an example of what was done to create different market niches in the egg industry. In this case, we disrupted a multibillion-dollar industry. Our success in the egg industry came from segmenting our products to different niches.

Case Study: Egg Industry

Methodology

I will be commenting on the takeaways from the focus groups of Martha Guidry's Consumer Reactions. Martha was a Proctor & Gamble graduate and an expert in market research and later a talented board advisor. It was her research that helped create a multibillion-dollar industry through smart segmentation and skuification. The focus group discussion started at the early stages of the project, and as the business began to grow, we had scaling discussions for improvement.

There were two one-hour focus groups conducted in Hackensack, New Jersey. The location was selected based on its proximity to several ShopRite Inserra stores in which Radlo Foods desired a test market.

We recruited respondents using the following criteria:

- Female head of household twenty-five to fifty-four years of age
- Must be responsible for at least 50 percent of the household grocery shopping
- Must do the majority of their grocery shopping at ShopRite
- Must purchase eggs most often from ShopRite
- Must purchase at least two dozen eggs a month
- Must purchase brand-name or premium/specialty eggs most often
- At least two people in each group must have purchased a bonus pack in the past three months

Qualitative research is only directional and cannot be used to predict the opinion of the population at large. The findings accurately represent the opinion of those individuals who attended the discussions. Use qualitative research to clarify existing theories, creating hypotheses and providing direction to future market research.

Objectives

- To identify the key motivations of egg-purchasing behavior
- Gain an understanding of the relative appeal of various egg positionings and concept elements as potential product claims
- Gain an understanding of communication priorities for packaging
- Determine interest level for alternative packaging and freshness/traceability etching

Key Findings

The egg category has many different brands and types of products. There are different claims on the packaging. Most of the women in the research study had little understanding of the various claims made on egg packaging. In general, they purchased what they typically bought from the egg case in their local grocery store. They didn't spend much time making decisions. Most of the participants didn't want a litany of claims on the package.

Those buying branded or premium eggs generally purchased a particular type based on what they believed it offered to them as a benefit. Many of them didn't completely understand the benefit they were purchasing but felt psychologically better for doing it. This train of thought was particularly true of those purchasing Omega 3 and Cage Free eggs. Those that were diehard Organic product purchasers felt they were getting the typical Organic product benefits by doing so.

The three major positioning ideas, Cage Free, Organic, and Omega 3, were all appealing to a subsection of our shoppers. Generally, specific consumers were attracted to one of the three concepts but not all of them. In other words, a Cage Free shopper doesn't necessarily want an Organic product and vice versa.

The No Antibiotics claim was considered somewhat appealing but less important than its sister claim, No Growth Hormones. Although Organic seemed to include these two claims, No Growth Hormones was considered a more vital claim. Also, not everyone felt that Organic as a standalone concept appealed to

them, but No Growth Hormones was relevant to most.

The All Natural claim was polarizing but intriguing because it had a different meaning to consumers. The vagueness of the claim made it unappealing to some, as previously mentioned. The broad territory this covered opened an opportunity for the Born Free line of eggs.

Vague claims or positioning were often not appealing. In some cases, once the claims were clarified, such as Vegetarian becoming Vegetarian Fed, it became more intriguing. Claims that were considered only moderately attractive because of a vague understanding included Free Roaming Hens and All Natural.

Several claims were considered weak or confusing and unnecessary. These included: No Chicken Molting, Naturally Raised, USDA Certified Organic, Whole Grain, and No Animal Byproducts. Generally, claims that encompassed numbers and statistics were disliked. This type of claim included information such as the milligrams of Omega 3 or DHA in an egg.

Brand name and egg type were the essential communication pieces on the package based on the shelf purchase decision process. The size of the egg was secondary, which was then followed by egg color, quantity, and expiration date. Some of the participants had packaging preferences, but this was often dictated by their choice of the brand initially selected.

Packaging

Most consumers focus on the product they are purchasing inside of the packaging. How a product is displayed and how easy it is to store and handle are essential characteristics of the product's attractiveness to consumers as well. The packaging is part of the selling proposition. Marketing research for packaging is a critical component of the process before going to market.

In the egg case study, considerations for the packaging included:

- How the customers shopped for eggs
- How much time the customers spent viewing the product on the shelf
- The durability of the packaging
- The benefit claims that drew attention to the value of the product

We observed purchasing interests based on a variety of package designs.

From the packaging designs that we tested for the eggs, the clear plastic carton option was well liked for several attributes. It was a favorite for the majority of participants. We received feedback that it appeared to be high quality, consumer friendly, could be safely transported, and was considered to be easily recyclable. Another favorite carton option was the Double Decker bonus pack. It was easy to store in the refrigerator, and broken eggs were visible without opening the package.

We presented the participants with eggs that had etchings on the shell. This option received mixed reviews. The participants were not intrigued by the applications suggested for the use of this technology. They were unable to see a viable consumer benefit.

Recommendations

After reviewing the data collected from our packaging research, we decided to focus on the Born Free and possible specialty private label lines for the three primary consumer appealing positionings: Organic, Omega 3, and Cage Free. We eliminated the Cage Free Organic since the Organic and the Cage Free consumers were looking for different benefits in addition to our nutritionally enhanced egg, Egg-Land's Best partnership.

We eliminated sub-brands with confusing descriptors. Consumers didn't understand Whole Grain or Vegetarian as standalone ideas. We added an All Natural SKU, which focused on areas such as No Growth Hormones without saying Organic and Vegetarian Fed. Further research was suggested before a full-scale launch. We created All Natural Vegetarian Fed eggs.

We placed information and education for the identification of the benefits of the three consumer-appealing positionings on the packaging. The package copy and design elements aligned with the consumer's shelf purchase decision process and communication hierarchy. We eliminated low-impact claims. The clear plastic carton was consistent with an upscale branded product. We continued the development of the Double Decker bonus pack because consumers showed that they liked the variety.

We decided to revisit the studies showing consumer appeal of etching and traceability and dating right on the eggs. These qualitative findings seemed inconsistent with our prior learning. The previous quantitative study we conducted may not have reflected the branded/premium egg purchaser that we interviewed. In the end, the retailers loved this idea, so we pursued it.

Habits and Practices

In our research, respondents were buying anywhere from two to six dozen eggs per month. For most, this meant they were at the dairy case, making a purchase decision two to four times a month. Eggs were considered a staple, like milk, so they always wanted to have a dozen on hand. Most of the typical egg consumption was for eating, rather than baking.

Respondents purchased branded or specialty eggs instead of the generic retailer brand for a variety of reasons:

- Taste – Most believed that branded/specialty eggs tasted better for individual consumption compared to a ShopRite egg.

- Eating habit of a family member – If a particular dietary restriction or situation was indicated, like Vegetarian or Organic, then a specialty egg was often selected.

- Added health benefit – Specific eggs were chosen because they offered a perceived benefit, such as Omega 3.

- Eggs are in better condition – Many said that the generic eggs were often cracked and in bad condition. The assumption was that a branded egg producer was in the egg business, not the grocery business, so they would handle and package the eggs better.

The retailer generic eggs were often purchased for the following reasons:

- There was a good sale.

- There was a large amount of baking to be done.

- There was an individual who ate them that wouldn't notice a difference.

Some of the respondents said that the generic large eggs were bigger than the branded ones, so they would likely choose them for baking. Recipes typically call for

Extra Large eggs. The branded eggs tended to be smaller.

When observing the color choice between brown or white eggs, respondents rarely would switch. Most stated that they were raised on a particular color egg or their children would only eat a specific color. The majority didn't know why eggs were in different colors. Many theories were raised: the chicken feed, the type of chicken, and the environment in which the chicken was raised, since all Cage Free eggs seemed to be brown. A few thought that brown eggs were supposed to be healthier, as they were more "country-like." Despite these theories, most felt that white and brown eggs tasted the same.

Most people buy Large eggs for general use and Extra Large for cooking since recipes often specify Extra Large. Most thought that Extra Large and Jumbo were the same size egg. Most assumed the egg size was related to the size of the hen, but they weren't sure. This information led us to skuify by size and sell for general use and cooking use, justifying the addition of another size on the shelf. Jumbo and Extra Large both sold well.

Most respondents were aware that they shouldn't keep the eggs on the refrigerator door due to temperature variations. As a result, many kept the eggs in the carton. This situation had implications for the package in terms of accessibility and viewability. Most referred to the expiration on the container to determine freshness, since they kept the cartons. Virtually all the women said they usually used up all the eggs before the expiration date, but if they passed the date, a few would throw them away.

Several respondents mentioned that they thought the generic eggs were fresher than the branded eggs because they turned faster due to the lower price point. Often, the generic egg area was near empty, while the branded and specialty eggs were fully stocked. Most felt that there wasn't a massive difference in price for the generic eggs versus the branded/premium eggs. They thought that the better taste or unique benefit (Organic, Omega 3) was worth an extra thirty to forty cents per carton.

Generally, sales and promotions didn't change the purchase behavior of the respondents unless they needed a large volume of eggs for non-eating purposes. The respondents said they'd often buy the cheap eggs for Easter (to color) or Halloween (to throw). A few were influenced by the buy one, get one free deal with ShopRite, rather than a sale price. Promotions increased purchasing by 30 to 50 percent.

EGG CONCEPT ELEMENTS | Chart 1.1

"Life stage"	Stronger Ideas	Moderate Ideas	Weaker Ideas
How Hen Treated on Farm	Cage Free	Free Roaming Hens All Natural (?)*	No Chicken Molting Naturally Raised
How Hen is Fed	Organic No Growth Hormones	All Natural (?)* No Antibiotics Vegetarian [Fed]**	USDA Organic Certified Organic Whole Grain No Animal By-Products
Egg Composition	Omega 3	All Natural (?)*	200mg Omega 3 600mg Omega 3 75mg DHA per egg

Cage Free and Free Roaming Hens

The most compelling hen treatment claim was Cage Free, and it appealed to a particular consumer group. To most, this communicated humane treatment of the hen. Many of the respondents assumed that if the hens weren't locked up in a pen and were able to move around, they would be healthier. They thought they would lay better-tasting eggs. Besides, they felt if the hens weren't caged, then they probably wouldn't spread sickness as easily, thus needing fewer antibiotics. A few said that it felt psychologically better to know the hens were able to move around more freely. This thought process segues into humane nation segmentation.

The free roaming hens' message was interpreted somewhat similarly to Cage Free, but it raised fears. Respondents felt it suggested poor oversight and management. They were concerned that the farmer wouldn't notice as quickly if the hens were eating well or if their health had deteriorated. Respondents didn't want eggs from underfed or unhealthy hens.

A few respondents didn't want to think about the daily life of the hens. The Free Roaming and Cage Free claims reminded them of the egg lifecycle, which they didn't want to consider. The few that found the claims unappealing viewed the eggs as a significant food source from a factory-like farm. They understood the chickens weren't merrily hopping around on a farm. The respondents weren't against the claims, but the claims didn't influence their purchase decision. They were not interested in this information.

All Natural

The term All Natural was confusing to respondents; the variety of interpretations meant that any execution of the concept would need to take a specific positioning for believability. The vagueness of this concept without supporting information made it unappealing. The standalone idea of All Natural didn't communicate enough to the consumer. All Natural encompassed all three egg life stages, but respondents weren't able to link the term to a specific end benefit for themselves.

Some of the respondents thought it described the treatment of the hen. They thought it meant something like Cage Free, where the hen was raised in a more natural setting. Others felt it meant No Antibiotics/ No Growth Hormones. On the other hand, some feared that All Natural communicated that a sick hen would receive no medical treatment. There was also some confusion about the egg composition. One woman stated, "What's unnatural about an egg? I don't get it." The All Natural claim made her question what she already understood about an egg.

Naturally Raised

The term Naturally Raised was confusing, so most found that it didn't influence their purchase decision. Some felt it meant the hen was raised the way a chicken is supposed to be raised—on a farm. Others thought it meant Free Roaming or that the claim referred to the hen's feed not having additives. The vagueness of the claim made it unconvincing. Naturally Raised did not mean the same thing as All Natural for most of the respondents. Although Naturally Raised was described similarly, the individuals did not reach the same conclusion for both claims.

No Chicken Molting

The respondents didn't understand the No Chicken Molting claim and thus viewed it as irrelevant. A few said that it sounded like something bad was happening to the chicken. Others noted that chickens naturally molt, so the claim was confusing. We explained that the concept could mean Cruelty-Free or Humane Practices. A few respondents said that there were probably more effective, straightforward ways to communicate this.

Organic / No Growth Hormones / No Antibiotics

Many respondents were interested in the concept of Organic or at least the communication of the claims they perceived as being Organic, No Antibiotics, and No Growth Hormones. The consensus was respondents wanted to know that nothing that entered the chicken's body would be passed into the egg. An Organic egg was considered more natural because it was free of pesticides and drugs. Respondents were more concerned with the growth hormones than the antibiotics. The concern was growth hormones in food sources could contribute to children physically maturing faster. Several women expressed optimism that farmers would remove sick hens, so antibiotics weren't essential. Others accepted the use of antibiotics as long as they were only treating the sick hens and not all of them unnecessarily.

Some of the respondents perceived Organic as a much more encompassing term than any of the other proposed claims. They considered Organic to be a lifestyle, not just a way to treat a food source. For these respondents, anything Organic was appealing, and the price wasn't a barrier. A few were skeptical of the Organic claim. They acknowledged Organic eggs would never be in their consideration set. They didn't trust that someone wasn't just putting a stamp on it and charging more money. They felt that the Organic boom was hype. They weren't willing to pay twice the price for an Organic product.

The claims of Certified Organic and USDA Organic didn't provide any additional reassurance or benefit to most consumers. Most felt that if a product was Organic, it was certified by some agency, and it didn't need the additional verbiage. Based on the responses, we felt USDA Organic added more credibility because it was a familiar government agency. We

also found that respondents that liked the Organic products weren't necessarily interested in the Cage Free claims. This discovery had implications for the Born Free SKU lineup.

Vegetarian Fed and No Animal Byproducts

When reviewing the Vegetarian Fed and No Animal Byproducts claims, respondents felt the claim of Vegetarian was confusing and as a result became less impactful. Some thought that the claim referred to the hen laying the egg, while others thought it meant that the egg was acceptable for a vegetarian diet. When probed further, Vegetarian Fed was more compelling. It clarified the confusion as to whether it referred to the hen or the consumer. That being said, only some respondents found knowing the feed type relevant to the quality of an egg. Many respondents didn't want to think that specifically about the process.

We found that the claim Vegetarian Fed was more compelling than No Animal Byproducts. Like the sister claim, most respondents were confused by the standalone claim of No Animal Byproducts. Vegetarian Fed seemed consistent with what respondents felt a hen should be eating, rather than a claim presenting the absence of a negative.

One respondent from a Kosher home said it didn't matter what the chicken ate or else all eggs wouldn't be Kosher. If the feed truly affected the egg, then any egg from a chicken that was fed pork would not be Kosher. To her knowledge, there wasn't a non-Kosher egg available.

Whole Grain

When reviewing the Whole Grain concept, none of the respondents had positive feedback. They felt it was irrelevant information about an egg. Similar to the Vegetarian and No Animal Byproduct claims, they didn't know if the claim referred to the feed or something else. Most respondents thought that Whole Grain referred to a type of bread and had no place being an egg type or sub-brand. A few said that if Whole Grain linked to a benefit such as better taste or improved digestion, then it might have meaning. As a standalone idea, it was meaningless. Most respondents assumed Whole Grain resulted in a brown egg due to the association with whole grain bread. A white egg would not make sense to them with this concept.

Omega 3 and DHA

The idea of an Omega 3 egg was appealing to some of the respondents, despite not knowing what the benefit was. Some understood that Omega 3 was supposed to improve brain and heart health, but most associated it with fish. Others didn't eat fish, so they felt they would receive some benefit from the egg. One of the respondents stated, "It feels like a bonus if I get a little into my family."

Some didn't understand if the Omega 3 egg was enriched or if it was naturally occurring. Their lack of understanding made it a less appealing idea. The respondents felt that if they wanted Omega 3, they'd eat more fish or take a vitamin; they wouldn't look to an egg to provide it. Some respondents wanted to know what they were doing to the egg to get the Omega 3 in it.

None of the respondents wanted to know how many milligrams of Omega 3 were in the egg. Seeing a number made them wonder if the egg had enough or too much, causing them to question what was in the egg. Those that liked the concept assumed the amount of Omega 3 was enough in the egg, and there wasn't a need for the amount to be labeled. A few said that if the farms wanted to put the milligrams, then it needed a recommended daily allowance (RDA) context. No one knew what the RDA was for Omega 3. None of the respondents were familiar with the Christopher Egg, with six hundred milligrams of Omega 3. They didn't think six hundred milligrams were more convincing than two hundred milligrams. It was vital for us to see that the amount wasn't crucial to the effectiveness of the claim.

Respondents didn't understand the claim for DHA because they didn't know its benefit. To them, it was an unnecessary claim.

Specialty and premium egg purchasers said they spent only a few seconds making a decision when they approached the shelf. The hierarchy of information needs was reasonably consistent across all the shoppers. They first identified the brand or the egg type when they approached the shelf. This information was critical to determine if they were getting what they wanted. Secondly, respondents wanted to make sure they had the right size egg. Most consumers were looking for Large eggs. Next, they chose by color, quantity, and expiration date. The package type was generally the last selection element, but it was often predetermined based on the choice of the brand or type in the first area of their decision process.

The clear plastic carton was well liked for several attributes and a favorite for the majority of participants. Most respondents liked that they could see all the eggs to determine if they were broken without opening the carton. Respondents thought the additional plastic cover on the top of the eggs would reduce cracks to the shells. Some liked how they could easily see how many eggs were in the carton without opening it when the eggs were on their home refrigerator shelf. Most of them felt that the plastic was easily recycled.

The clear plastic carton only edged out the Styrofoam carton for being recyclable and being slightly higher quality. Several respondents felt that they would open the container to look at the eggs in the store, even with a clear view package. The one-hinge versus two-hinge design with a locking device was easier to open to check eggs. Some respondents wanted to reach into the carton without pulling

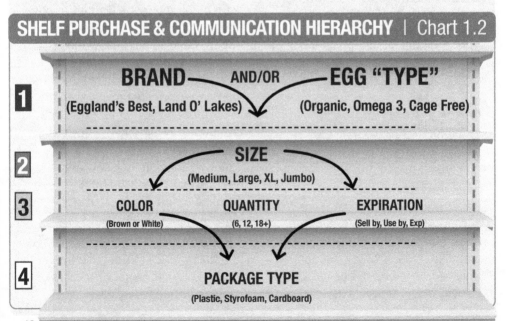

SHELF PURCHASE & COMMUNICATION HIERARCHY | Chart 1.2

1 BRAND — AND/OR — EGG "TYPE"
(Eggland's Best, Land O' Lakes)   (Organic, Omega 3, Cage Free)

2 SIZE
(Medium, Large, XL, Jumbo)

3 COLOR   QUANTITY   EXPIRATION
(Brown or White)   (6, 12, 18+)   (Sell by, Use by, Exp)

4 PACKAGE TYPE
(Plastic, Styrofoam, Cardboard)

it out of the refrigerator, and they could not do that with the three-fold plastic carton. A few of them felt that the Styrofoam container was higher quality than the clear plastic due to this perceived extra padding for safer transport.

As for the cardboard packaging, respondents felt it was old-fashioned. It was the carton their "mother used." Also, some perceived the cardboard as more challenging to cut down to a half dozen if they wanted to conserve space in their refrigerator.

Value-Added Ideas

Respondents liked the Double Decker value pack and considered it unique. Some of them felt that it would take less room in their refrigerator, and the two packs could be easily separated if necessary.

Most of them thought that they could view all the eggs for breakage due to the clear plastic carton. They also perceived eight free eggs on the top of the carton as a good value, but most of the respondents wanted to "do the math."

Respondents perceived eighteen-packs as a more typical value pack. Although a bonus pack could fall into their consideration set when they needed a high volume of eggs (holiday baking, Easter eggs, etc.), sometimes a higher need resulted in them purchasing a cheaper product. Their price benchmark was often not with their typical high-end product when deciding on the purchase.

Egg Etching Reviews

Respondents that liked the concept of egg etching felt that it would be easier to rotate their eggs to know which ones needed to be used up first. Those who found it less appealing kept their eggs in the carton in their refrigerator. They felt that the date/code on the carton was adequate for knowing the expiration date and any recall issues.

Photo 1.A

When probed for specific etching applications, respondents were not particularly enthusiastic, as noted below:

· **Freshness Dating** – Most respondents felt that the expiration date on the package was adequate, and the eggs were generally used before the expiration date. When asked about a "born on" or "laid on" date to communicate better freshness, most didn't feel they wanted to think about the egg-laying process.

· **Traceability** – The results were similar to the freshness dating. Most felt that the package coding was adequate.

· **Assurance You Are Getting What You Paid For** – Having a logo or Organic stamp was considered somewhat helpful to minimize the risk of switching, but respondents trusted both the egg farm and the grocer to be honest. Virtually all the respondents who switched eggs in stores to ensure that none were broken said they always switched them with the same kind.

· **Promotional Coding** – Most felt that if promotions were on the eggs, this would encourage more people to open the carton, handle the eggs, and switch them around, which they didn't find appealing.

Concerns were also raised about the etching process. Here were the responses:

· **Made Egg Seem Unnatural** – Many of the women felt that a sticker would be a better approach than the etching. The printing on the egg seemed unnatural and inconsistent with what an egg is all about. Many of these women bought Organic or Cage Free eggs, so the etching seemed out of alignment with their desired egg type.

· **Ink** – Most wanted to know what the ink was made of on the egg. Many feared that it was adding dyes or chemicals to what was a natural product. Since many of these respondents wanted No Growth Hormones and No Antibiotics, adding this unnatural print to the eggshell was counterproductive to that goal.

Etching: General Learning

In separate focus groups, we examined the etching in greater detail. We had what was making for an interesting dynamic. The male investors and buyers loved the etching. They thought it was unique as part of an overarching egg safety action plan where we had the safest and best egg in the country. Etching garnered support from Food Safety News and the general press.

There are goals you want to accomplish when launching a product or service, which include establishing trade relationships, brand presence, corporate presence, and credibility. In conjunction with achieving these goals were the manifestation of increased revenue, units, profits, and high growth.

We were using technology in all parts of our business: ag-tech, tech cartons, tech etching, tech food safety. This was positive from a trade perspective to make a strong run and get acceptance over a few years while we had the "new mousetrap" that everyone would desire. We had a pipeline filled with new mousetraps to garner excitement and attention. At the same time, we knew the long game was disruption through wholesomeness, health, animal welfare, and sustainability, but with technological support for the long game.

Meanwhile, we went from a test market to moving towards a few dozen states of distribution. Some technological edges like the plastic cartons work well long-term, as does the nutraceutical feed additive technology. We fed hens Omega 3 through a variety of sources to get the tested level, as well as the other ingredients in the Born Free, EB, and private label formulas.

We examined the great divide between the long-term woman primary and secondary target market shoppers and the trade. The divide was fine, as long as the big buzz didn't cause adverse customer complaints, loss of growth, or business.

Here are some further comments from the target women in the next consumer reactions focus group for the technological egg etching. We saw that etching was going to be a short-term buzz and not a long-term sticker.

The respondents that had noticed the etching thought the expiration date was helpful, but none would purposefully buy the eggs specifically for the etching. Many of them kept the eggs in the carton, so the sell-by date was adequate for their needs. Because the respondents typically used the eggs before the sell-by date, the expiration date became obsolete.

The tracking number didn't pique the respondents' interest because they didn't understand the purpose it would serve. Several mentioned that if they broke the eggshell, it would be difficult to read the code at that point, especially if it was the last egg in the box. Many of them felt that if they threw away the carton, the tracking code was useless because they wouldn't have an 800 number to call. The code didn't provide enough useful information.

Overall, most assumed that the etching was expensive, which raised the price of the egg. Many suggested that they'd rather eliminate the etching and receive a lower price.

Freshness and Safety

In regards to freshness of the eggs, most of the respondents used the sell-by date to determine freshness. Given that eggs are generally used quickly, few of them feared that their eggs weren't fresh. Overall, most of the respondents had never experienced a "bad egg," so they assumed that freshness wasn't a big concern.

When reviewing safety implications, most respondents were concerned with the handling and care of meat products rather than with any other types of products. Many felt that since an egg was in a sealed shell, there was little concern about contamination. For the most part, the respondents trusted that the eggs were appropriately handled throughout the production and distribution. Many of them cited standards set by the FDA that ensure safety in the US production of food goods. Respondents felt that the retailer might need the traceability code if there were consumer complaints about the product, since they'd bring the product back to the retailer with any issues.

Etched Egg Concept

Only a few of the respondents said the concept made them excited about buying an etched egg. The concept appealed to low volume purchasers who took the eggs out of the carton; they thought the date might be helpful to ensure the eggs were still good. Most knew the brand of eggs they had purchased, so they saw no value in having the brand name reinforced

on the egg. All respondents viewed the store as the place to bring back a questionable egg. If they had thrown out the carton, they wouldn't know who to call with a rotten egg based on the code.

Key Conclusions and Recommendations: Packaging

Through our research, we acquired the directional focus group information that we needed. We planned to push forward as long as we could to get our product into stores. Meanwhile, we had intentions beyond etching. We reviewed the packaging a few years later for consideration of updating it. We won awards and grew at double- and triple-digit rates with all of our brands, but we were focused on continual improvement as we started to scale growth with new technology regarding the packaging. Believe me, it was a difficult fight to get the suppliers to upgrade so we could fuel our specialty growth. The boys and girls in the fiberboard business had to upgrade with new machinery. Interplast plastic cartons from Montreal, Canada, had started to eat away at serious market share with their tri-fold carton. Nothing but significant loss of market share was going to make that happen.

Liquid Egg Launch: Not Every Launch Will Work

There was additional information for the liquid launch for the future. We had put quite a bit of money into the intellectual property and joint partnership with Cargill's CoroWise as well as with development help from Rose Acre Farms. This idea was board member Tony DeLio's, along with Marketing Director Joan Leroy's great product opportunity. I partnered on developing this intellectual property. We had just started marketing the CoroWise to one account when we exited the business.

What happened between the focus group and the launch of Heart Goodness® was a major consumer behavior shift with the advancement of cholesterol statin medicine such as Crestor. This effectively meant a change of needs for people as statins were greatly accepted. They no longer needed a cholesterol-reducing product because the statins were working so well. It's a challenge when you do new product development to get it right. We were also moving beyond our reach to take a small part of a large category. I should have killed the liquid segment at the outset because it was a small niche of a small market. I was drawn in by the partnership with Cargill and the prospects of hitting the market right so we could expand Heart Goodness into other marketing areas. The overall pie was not small, but we didn't see the behavior shift coming.

Typically, liquid eggs were purchased for adult-only usage, while shelled were for the children and specific meals such as a fried egg sandwich. Generally, parents didn't worry about cholesterol with their children, so they felt the shelled eggs were a better value because they were cheaper.

Usage of liquid eggs was generally driven by three needs:

- **Cholesterol** – Respondents were concerned about their cholesterol levels, so liquid eggs provided an easy solution.

- **Dietary requirements** – Respondents wanted egg whites because they contained less fat.

- **Convenience** – A quick and easy way to make French toast or bake when there was a shortage of time or eggs. Many froze the liquid eggs as a spare.

Overall, the respondents' perception was that liquid eggs were healthier because they had less yolk and were often enriched with Omega 3. Most respondents did not realize that Egg Beaters® was artificially colored and did not have any yolk. Interestingly, most purchased branded liquid eggs but were often indifferent to the shelled egg brand. The major difference was an egg had a shell that was a natural casing, so there were no concerns that something shouldn't be in the product. Respondents feared the contents of a store-brand liquid egg might not be as controlled. The Heart Goodness® name was well liked and transparent. It effectively communicated that the liquid egg would be healthy and good for the heart.

Two strong concepts were identified:

Concept T – The promise of heart health, combined with the familiarity of Omega 3 drove the appeal.

Concept P – This approach to the plant sterols was the most compelling of the two presented. Although most respondents wanted to know more about the additive, they were open to the benefit of reducing cholesterol. Some were wary of an unknown additive that they had not yet heard about in the media or in other products.

Note: additional work needed to be done to develop an appropriate consumer insight to prioritize the communication in the concept and to determine if too much education would be required to get consumers over the knowledge/ familiarity hurdle.

Summary

In the real world, you have to do research. It can be exceedingly helpful. It's not absolute, but speaking with the customer is crucial. The customer is king. From here, we developed the lineup in a Good, Better, and Best framework that disrupted a multibillion-dollar commodity industry with health and humane segmentation, new products, and packaging.

Development from Focus Groups and Market Research

The strategy of total attack and displacement of generic eggs on the shelf we coined as "skuification." This idea came from the focus groups, with every conceivable product and size put on the buyer's table for review. This was a heavy burden, but the strategy proved to be fruitful. Can you imagine the buyer's face when you throw dozens of packages on his or her desk?

They started with the throwaways with the bigger packages, and then they selected two or three to start. This technique beat the presentation of two options and winding up with zero. We pushed Good, Better, and Best in every conceivable way, including product features, size, type of packaging, color, and brand. In the end, we ended up with two major brands on the shelf, Egg-Land's Best and Born Free, with some instances of private label for the third.

We presented Best, Better, and Good in that order. Foam packaging was considered the Good option, an overlay as Better packaging, and plastic and china white fiberboard as the Best packaging. The Best color of an egg was brown. The Good color was white, and as part of the journey, we were able to work with the Tufts veterinary school and develop Anaconda Blue Green Eggs, which we called Better. It was a smaller volume,

GOOD BETTER BEST DIAGRAM | Chart 1.3

FEATURES

GOOD	BETTER	BEST
Vegetarian Fed	Omega	Eggland's Best Taste and Nutrition
Cage Free	Free Range	Pasture Raised | Organic

PACKAGING

GOOD	BETTER	BEST
Foam	Overlay	Plastic

Photo 1.B

SIZES

GOOD	BETTER	BEST
Small/Medium	Large/X-Large	Jumbo

EGG COLOR

GOOD	BETTER	BEST
White	Blue-Green	Brown

AMOUNT

GOOD	BETTER	BEST
18 Pack or Larger	Dozen	6 Pack

and Jesse and Jerry Laflamme at Pete and Gerry's were delighted to market it. Now, of course, Pete and Gerry's overall operation of it has turned into over $200 million in sales. On features, we had the Good as the Vegetarian Fed, the Better was Omega, and Best was Egg-Land's Best.

New products and trends continued to evolve so that when Cage Free emerged, we were already looking at a few years down the pike as to how we could incorporate Free Range and Pasture Raised as well as other value-added products. Down the pike, we had plans for hard-boiled eggs in a bag and liquid eggs with added properties. We were close to violating principles of a fast-growing segment of a large market, but the liquid eggs consumer was not a large segment. When considering the animal welfare concept later on, the Good option was Cage Free, the Better option was Free Range, and the Best option was Pasture Raised. However, that was not the case when we started the process, because we needed to get the Cage Free eggs on the shelf.

Looking at the options for sizing were as follows: The Good category was Small and Medium eggs, Better was Large and Extra Large eggs, and the Best was Jumbo eggs. Ironically, the best-tasting eggs come from small and medium-size hens. The Jumbo eggs come from older birds. Sometimes the taste isn't as appealing, and they also have thinner shells with more cracks. However, the perception was the reverse. We later used the same method when we came out with Fresh Eggs peeled in the bag and did so in each variety of Born Free and later Egg-Land's Best. It was another tremendous success.

We also marketed Organic Orange Juice, Humane Turkey, a Humane Dairy line featuring my daughter Jessica and a newly born baby cow, which my daughter named Ruthy, and other commodity-based agriculture products. We had some success with these products in the marketplace.

The sales team, along with the brokers, would place in Vegetarian Fed, Omega 3, Cage Free, Free Range, Organic, and Egg-Land's Best in every size, including Medium, Large, Extra Large, and Jumbo. We would, at times, need to balance the lack of Jumbos and the fact that Mediums did not sell that well, but were only a small portion of what the flocks laid. We had to watch the Jumbo sales because they were short as well, but much in demand. We would also skuify by type of package, size, and in addition to dozens, six-packs, eighteen-packs, thirty-packs, two-dozen-packs, fifteen dozen loose eggs without cartons in an appealing case, as well as thirty dozen loose eggs in an appealing case. As part of skuification, we would use different packaging for different reasons, including bright white, plastic, and pulp cartons with an overlay.

We did this to build a consumer billboard at point of purchase. We knew from our research that a consumer would spend about seven seconds at the egg case. If we could get them to stop at the specialty eggs, because of the amount and volume of choices, it was more likely that they would buy one of the higher-end selections. For the benefit of the consumer, we had rack pricing. I was never a fan of exceeding the magic number of $4.00 per unit in dairy and frankly rarely did so. Building in the retailer's margin, we would build a rack tier. Vegetarian Fed's goal was not more than $1.99 with a few cents more for Extra Large eggs, $2.49 for Omega Eggs, $2.99 for Cage Free, $3.29 for Free Range, and we looked to keep the Organic eggs under $4.00. Because Organic eggs cost more to produce, we favored a lower price but with a six-pack. In later years, we used similar cost structures with hard-boiled eggs in a pouch. We offered fewer eggs, accounting for the added cost and value of removing the shells and cooking them. Our dairy and other food items were also value-priced.

Lessons Learned

Your Organic product pipeline should be deep and fruitful. It should use some or a mix of social health and animal welfare sustainable factors, economic factors, and differentiated biotech and technology with your products, product formulations, and packaging. Don't be afraid to get customer feedback on a variety of new offerings, which should be plentiful with a few throwaways. Have a growth platform ample to execute with enough resources geared to proper, consistent planning and value propositions.

Your value proposition is the beginning and end goal to meet your customers' needs. The product or service needs to be priced right. It must have value and quality. It's also crucial that you can deliver 98.5 percent fulfillment. Promotion must appropriately be promoted to gain trial and usage. A fast-growing small market of a larger category will work. You will soon find out whether you have a profitable niche or a gigantic business.

Anyone can do this. The youngest test examples I have seen were high school students. A group of young men figured out how to get rid of fire with magnetic metamaterials and sound waves. I'll share more on this later. If high school students can create a new pie, you can too, with the right tools and inspiration.

SECTION 2

FUNDING

CHAPTER TWO

PRINCIPLE II: Design and Deliver a Pitch That Secures Funding.

A business pitch is a presentation put together to entice an investor or group of investors. The goal of your pitch is to secure funding to proceed with your value proposition so you can take it to the market. Some people may ask why you would create a pitch before the business plan. In my opinion, they should be done at the same time.

I just raised money and completed a provisional patent application with the fourteen-year-old high school students who created a way to get rid of fire with magnetic metamaterials and sound waves. None of them had ever taken a statement analysis or done accounting. I figured that with the money we raised, they could hire someone to do the business plan with them or spend the money for education on accounting, finance, and statement analysis. Yes, a business plan is required, but consider it Appendix A to Principle II if you'd rather have it that way.

When you create your pitch, I suggest two separate formats that may be intertwined at times. The pitch process is about getting investors to back people. It's not about backing products and markets. The first template you will find below was put forth in conjunction with Steve "Zam" Zamierowski, an outstanding business plan coach and judge at Tufts University. The template will assist you in crafting your proposal thoroughly. However, you must take into consideration the factors of human behavior as they relate to the STRONG Method found in *Pitch Anything* by Oren Klaff. You can incorporate the principles found in this book into other areas of your life. I have reviewed many pitch decks in my day, but I have seen these two both raise real money and garner real excitement. You can also take the concepts from STRONG and use them with the base pitch.

With this base method, you should have a ten-slide deck. This would include:

1. Title slide
2. Massive problem that requires addressing
3. Value proposition solution
4. Underlying magic
5. Your business model
6. Sales strategy
7. Competition
8. Management team
9. Basic financials
10. Current status and offer

SLIDE DECK EXAMPLE | Chart 2.1

SLIDE 1:
Title

Introduce yourself to establish credibility

Elevator Pitch
– Value Proposition

Next 9 slides supports it

SLIDE 2:
The Problem/Market Opportunity

What's the problem:
market opportunity

Who's got the problem:
target customer

How big is the problem:
market size

3

SLIDE 3:
Your Solution

What product or service have you created

How does is solve the problems

10X better than what's currently available

4

SLIDE 4:
Technology/Invention

What's the underlying invention or breakthrough | **Is it patentable or protectable** | **What are the barriers to entry**

Major obstacle you've overcome

5

SLIDE 5:
Business Model

How will you make money
- What will you sell
- How will you sell – channels of distribution

How will you build the business
- Where is the initial market opportunity?

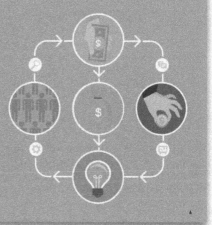

6

SLIDE 6:
Focused Go-To-Market Strategy

Who will be your first customers
- What market segment
- How will you find them
- How will you get their attention and time
- Why will they buy from **YOU**
- Why will they buy **NOW**

How will those first customers lead to more

7

33

SLIDE 7:
Competition

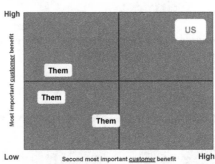

SLIDE 8:
Management Team (next 1-2 fundable events)

Management Team

How each of them are qualified to accomplish specific tasks to reach your next milestones

Advisory Team

Get industry leaders involved
- Affirmation
- Play key team roles

SLIDE 9:
Financial Projections (3 years)

- **Bottom Up, Not Top down**
- **Revenue = Units x ASP**
- **Costs include**
  - Head Count: fully loaded
- **Productivity assumptions**
  - COGS
  - Cost of sales and marketing (2-3x expected)
  - Capital equipment and G&A
- **Cash flow break even is not the main goal, being a market leader is.**
  - Selling price – COGS = Gross Margin

The specific numbers are less important than the assumptions!

SLIDE 10:

Status and Funding Requirement

- **Honest assessment of product/service readiness**
- **Honest customer feedback or sales**
- **Capital being sought**
  - Needs to take you to the next fundable milestone
- **What that capital will fund**
  - # months
  - Produce development
  - Key hires
  - Sales (# customers and revenue)

SLIDE 10A: NEED A FLOW-CHART TO SHOW USES OF CAPITAL BROKEN DOWN   11

SLIDE 11:

Ask for the Sale!

How will gaining the financing contribute to the success of your company.

– Get you to the next fundable milestone

12

There may be a few extra slides that may be used to enhance and individualize the presentation. This pitch method has been used quite successfully. Zwitterco successfully raised millions of dollars in the water pollution space. Medical delivery process space that requires FDA approval called Hero Patch. This method secured funding for a company in the Block Chain Space (SAAS & BAAS) called Beasy – Blockchain Made Easy. I have also seen it work for industries such as food, agriculture, nutrition, biotech, service, engineering, and nonprofits. It works for mature businesses in venture capital, a family office, and private equity opportunities. I have used this format to scale a small venture/private equity fund into a large one. It is industry agnostic in that respect, where specific slides can be modified to drive home key deliverables.

You are welcome to go to https://achievemost.com/ principles-of-cartel-disruption/ to attain examples of the Zwitterco and Hero Patch's presentation as well as attain other valuable resources.

Sup. 2.1

It doesn't matter whether you are a pre-revenue development company of patents, with technology, a drug that is being developed, or a traditional EBITDA (Earnings Before Interest, Taxes, Depreciation, and Amortization) business. The key is providing milestones, deliverables, value, and the finance needed to get there. It's also about making sure that the investor gets a return on their investment.

You want to be able to show a breakeven at twenty-four to thirty-six months or significant milestones achieved that go right to a multiple of X on value. Usually, on more substantial investments, 2X to 5X is sufficient for over three to seven years. With private equity returns, there is an expectation of growth at 18 to 30 percent. With a venture, there is a higher risk, so you are looking at 15X to 35X and beyond. When I say X, I mean a multiple for an investor, so if they put in $100, 5X would be $500. I am conveying basic expectations. The investors know that whatever numbers you come up with, you will likely be wrong. This is hard to say, but being upfront is essential. "We are asking for $350,000 now, and we know the projections that we gave may be wrong and will need to be adjusted." Be straightforward and show that you have done your analysis and revisit it often. The same would be true for billion-dollar projects.

Pitch Anything Recap

The second item that you need to learn is to present your pitch with the weapons and tactics from Oren Klaff's book *Pitch Anything*. I suggest reading the entire book. You have to understand what drives human beings' behavior in sales and in a pitch situation.

Klaff explains how our brains have evolved. First, the old brain, or crocodile brain, as he calls it, developed millions of years ago to process fight-or-flight responses to keep us alive. The croc brain filters from a basic survival level. If the information is not needed, it is disregarded.

Croc Brain Filters:

1. If it is not dangerous, ignore it.

2. If it is not new and exciting, ignore it.

3. If it is new, summarize it as quickly as possible, and forget about the details.

4. Do not send anything up to the neocortex for problem-solving unless you have a situation that is really unexpected and out of the ordinary.[1]

Pitches tend to originate from the neocortex of the brain, the problem-solving area, but are received by the croc brain that filters the importance of information. The croc brain looks for concrete evidence and not nuances. If you give too many details, the croc brain will discard or ignore your information. Your message must be simple to get through to the croc brain. You need an emotional story so that it's memorable. Also, you have to command attention through social status. Finally, you can't appear desperate or needy. Set the scenario so they come to you. Klaff suggests to pitch it STRONG: "Set the frame, Tell the story, Reveal the intrigue, Offer the prize, Nail the hook point, and Get the deal."[2]

Once you understand how the brain works, it's time to take frame control. A frame is an instrument you use to gain power, authority, strength, and control in your business communication. If your frame wins, your ideas will be accepted, but if it fails, you are at the mercy of the other person. Pitching is about being the alpha and the leader. If you're the beta and follower, you lose. Understanding how to apply power frames is one of the most important skills you will learn in business.

When you pitch, always finish early. If it is a group pitch or you are in competition with others, practice a dead-on finish of thirty seconds early at least. If you go over, you lose. Never present more than twenty minutes. I reviewed a pitch from a very prestigious senior executive whose firm was considered to be iconic in the management consulting and venture industry. Everyone was afraid to tell him the truth about why he was not getting the funding. He went on for forty-five slides and an hour and ten minutes in length. I told him the truth: I lost interest and most humans would after the twenty-minute point. He appreciated the candor and nailed his next financing trip.

When I was running for State Representative coming out of college, I was in hot pursuit of raising at least $35,000 to make a formidable challenge. I met with some potential supporters that were concerned about how a 21 year old could effectively compete for office. It was an added burden that there could be no corporate money involved. I sat down and respectfully listened to all the reasons why they shouldn't support me financially. I knew from research who they endorsed. After their speech, as I turned to leave, I challenged them. I wanted to know if candidate A or candidate B had knocked on 10,000 doors. Had either candidate organized a group of 50 volunteers to drop 50,000 pieces of literature? Had either of them put in 20% of the total money they needed as skin in the game and received initial political senior backing that matched the contribution? Then, I disrupted their power frame and said, "Could you kindly take a check out of your right drawer and write me a $2,000 check from your family now?"

Smiles appeared on their faces because this 21 year old had the guts and determination to approach the situation in this manner. I received multiple checks for $1,000 and a price break on a great campaign office, which was an upgrade from my home. You need to be the alpha, not the beta. You need to garner attention and respect. If you are the beta, you lose in a pitch. You have to be the prize. You deserve attention and respect. People want what they can't have, so they place the value on what's challenging to get.

When you pitch, be dynamic. Create curiosity and desire. Make the buyer qualify himself to do business with you. Protect your status when it comes to changing agendas, meeting times, or who will attend. Understand that being strong is important, and it is not about money. Your time is limited. You require respect, attention, and status before anyone is going to invest in you and your ideas.

If you go to an investor or customer's office, be prompt or early. Hold the expectation that your investor or customer be on time as well. Don't let yourself get beta trapped by having to wait for extended periods in the lobby. Your time needs to be respected. It's your responsibility to hold this boundary.

Twenty Minute STRONG Format

Whenever possible, I want the meeting to be on your turf. Having a meeting in your office gives you the upper hand. When it comes to presenting a pitch, I don't go to a coffee house for cold analytical meetings unless I want to be cold and analytical. Still, it is an incrementally better environment at times than the target's office.

When the meeting starts, introduce yourself. Give your background and the big idea within the first five minutes. Be straightforward.

My name is Joe Johnson. I went to Northeastern University. I hit quota in sales two years straight for Gogles-New Nutrition Tech. I learned financial analysis at night and finished off my master's degree in nutrition combined with an Innovation Management graduate degree at Tufts University. I left Gogles-New Nutrition Tech to start at this great opportunity.

The Big Idea

Before you pitch your big idea, set the stage by letting your audience know why now is the right time for your value proposition. What are the social, economic, or technology trends in business? The listener wants to know your idea is new and relevant. Let's go back to the wildfire example.

"For people that are looking for a better and effective way to fight the scourge of wildfires, my product is based on new technology by using low-frequency soundwaves and metamaterials to provide the ability to extinguish fires without water. Just imagine the economic and sustainable applications of replacing water with metamaterials and sound waves." (Specific applications may be cited as well.)

The pitch should be quick and to the point. The key in this part of the pitch are the technological factors of improvement in social sustainability and economic feasibility. It can be reasonably priced and has the potential to start as a niche that grows rapidly in a large market of fire protection.

Explain the Budget and Your Unfair Advantage: Ten Minutes

It's harder to hold attention in this part of the presentation but get through it sharply. Create your presentation with great graphics and visuals to tell the story. Keep in mind that human beings have short attention spans. The visuals will assist with the engagement of the viewers.

Be sure to cover the numbers and projections. Flowcharts are helpful to show you know what to spend along the way. Your audience knows you will be asking for a large amount of money and promising they will make it back in the future. *Unrealistic budgets and miscalculating costs are the greatest risks to a growing company, especially startups.*[3]

EXAMPLE:

$75,000 for patent lawyers

$50,000 for finish-off phase and commercialization of the product

$2,000 per month for facility lease x 24-month commitment = $48,000

$80,000 for additional research

You can use a deck for the business plan by citing it as an exhibit. It would cite the pitch numbers and projections. Typically, there will be a loss of money in the first thirty months. The loss is expected until a break-even point is reached. Then, as the business is scaled, you will tend to hit milestones. Be honest about the milestone projections. If you are pitching to grow a particular tree fruit in California, it may take nine years to see profits. Don't mislead your investors to believe there with be a return sooner. Focus on the milestones during that period that are key markers of success.

Show that you understand your business and that you know what it needs to succeed. Investment guys and gals have their check sheets. Strategic operating executives like myself can pick out great talent we'd like to quarterback in a business. A flowchart gives comfort to investors that if something doesn't go as planned, they won't have to overinvest in the beginning. They want to see you put considerable thought into the requirements to make your venture successful. This also leads to more thoughtful questions later when they are close to writing a check. The same is true for a larger business that has reached an inflection point and needs capital to scale facilities to get to the next level in terms of capacity to meet sales projections and their pipeline. Be sure to lay out what is needed. Explain the *what* and *why* for the cash requirements.

Be sure to communicate your competitive edge or unfair advantage you have over the competition. In the fire example, you have a patent pending, and it is your unique idea. How quickly can someone copy this? Determine how easy it would be for new competitors to get into the business and compete against you. What are the barriers to entry? Patents? Trademarks? Trade secrets? Size of competition and quickness of potential response? What is the time to go to market? It would be best if you had something unique to keep the attention of your potential investors.

Offer the Deal: Two Minutes

What is the audience going to receive when they do a deal with you? Be brief, rich, and high level.

"You get to be on this exciting, groundbreaking "new mousetrap" and get in on the ground floor" or "We are at an inflection point where we have the revenue but need cash for more production to support the revenue" or "We have this great new private equity fund dedicated to nutrition technologies that is showing 55 percent Segment Category Growth (CAGR) with a guaranteed 10 percent annual return."

Tell the audience what you will be delivering to them, when it will be delivered, and how.[4]

The Close: Three Minutes

Targets can like your deal and be willing to say yes or no before fully understanding it. We tend to like or dislike things before we know much about them. You want to avoid your audience slipping into cold, reasoned analysis paralysis and unemotional judgment of you and your ideas. It's like going on a first date for coffee versus going for a meal, ice cream, and a walk. A coffee date will end up with an analytical review of all of your weaknesses instead of a relaxed or exciting experience through intrigue, prizing, time frame, and moral authority.

People want to know how you have faced obstacles and overcome them. They want to see you in a situation that drives interesting people in whatever area of your involvement. They want to be with the strong. Don't look or be weak! And please eliminate the word "hope" from your pitches. "Hope" is not an effective strategy and makes you look weak. Throughout your pitch, maximize every word that you say in short sound bites so you don't bore the croc brain. Intrigue or excitement builds because of market forces, prizing, the time frame to get a decision, and moral authority. Get your point across quickly and win the deal!

CHAPTER THREE

PRINCIPLE III: Understand the Basic Legal Game, Documents for Funding, & Intellectual Property Protection.

Lawyers are the fabric of American society. I personally owe a debt of gratitude to some of the best lawyers in the world that have bailed me out of difficult situations. If I had known then what I know now about the legal profession and legal strategy, I would not have paid them the millions that I have had to throughout the years. One semester of business law in business school only skims the surface of what you need to know to protect yourself. It should be an expectation that you will be sued somewhere in the process. Everything you write in text or email could be subject to a lawsuit. Everything!

I have followed the credo of Great Uncle Boris Kostelanetz, a famous tax attorney and New York State Bar Association President, who once told me, "Lawsuits are for lawyers . . . stay the hell away from them if you can." Never once have I initiated a lawsuit unless another party has maliciously pursued us.

Lawyers go to school for three years and have a system set up for both billable hours and contingency that favors them in legal matters. You will likely be sued for one of the following: fraud, breach of contract, tortious interference, negligent misrepresentation, breach of fiduciary duties, employment issues, and scrutiny from regulators. If you are in business, you will be sued.

Lawsuits or threatening a lawsuit is a strategy. That is why the phrase "scorch and burn" was created; thank you, General Sherman. Big companies have the financial resources to fight and push out lawsuits. The fight starts the minute you've been served. That's why people hide under their desks when a third-party constable or process server attempts to serve the lawsuit. I am not an attorney. I am not giving legal advice, but I suggest you study up on the following terms and speak to a litigating attorney: quash service, motion to dismiss, summary judgment, jurisdiction in a lawsuit, waive a trial and go for mandatory arbitration, waive a trial by jury. Those subjects weren't taught in the one-semester business-law class in business school. When you get sued, it will benefit you to know what these are in advance. Former Massachusetts Bar Association President Chris Kenney and his partners are excellent litigating attorneys. There are many others out there.

It's critical to hire great legal counsel to prevent you from getting into trouble. The best deal in the world is the one that your attorney keeps you from entering. You will also need attorneys to matriculate deals, such as outstanding attorneys Kitt Sawitsky and Greg Getschman of Goulston & Storrs, who steered the author through some perilous times, whether in start-up mode, in growth, securities issues, and into larger companies. Advice will be required along the way.

Start-Up Early Stage Venture

In the early stages of a start-up, the rule of thumb is generally to self-finance first along with applying for grants. Next, you can go to friends and family for financing. When that is exhausted, move on to investor financing. When you go to the final group of people, you don't know their level of comfort, and you might not know who their partners are, but having financing will be your lifeblood. To borrow a phrase from SoBe founder and current Reed's beverage chairman John Bello, "Vision without money is insanity."

Intellectual property (IP) includes your original ideas, inventions, designs, discoveries, and creative work. You must protect your IP. This ensures your ideas won't be stolen. Some law firms will defer the cost of patents and start-up expenses until after your fundraising occurs. Doug Kline, a senior partner at Goodwin Procter, is one such attorney that works with representing technology and life science companies involved in IP. His partners include Joel Lehrer and Mitzi Chang, who handle high-prospective start-up technology ventures. If vetted positively, you can get a break on terms. Cash flow is king in the early stages of a venture. An eighteen-month delay in legal fees is highly beneficial, or any delay along with a possible cap on fees. It also gives an attorney some skin in the game.

There are generally two ways of financing a start-up venture. One way is a SAFE instrument—not to be confused with SAFE, LLC, those great high school students from New Hampshire who won the Conrad Challenge at NASA in 2018—and the other is a convertible note (CVN). SAFE stands for a Simple Agreement for Future Equity. It is not an instrument used for debt. A CVN is a type of debt that converts to equity in the company. According to Goodwin Procter, SAFE instruments are used more on the West Coast, while a CVN is more prevalent on the East Coast.

For entrepreneurs, the focus should be to raise capital. Decisions should be made with a competent member of the legal profession. Decide whether you want to have a valuation cap, discount offer, interest, and rights to invest at pro rata or later rounds. The purpose of a valuation cap is that investors have a minimum amount of equity that they will receive on the transactions.

So what's my personal favorite? It doesn't matter, but I will tell you what an investor likes the best. They want a guaranteed piece of the rock, meaning equity shares or convertible equity shares, discounts for additional investing, and discounts for investing now, as well as opportunities to invest in future rounds and interest on their money. Once you start growing, you can usually get most venture capitalists to kick in when the growth exceeds 40 percent of combined EBITDA and YOY (Year on Year) Growth. You might also gain their interest when the minimum revenue threshold, $4 million, for example, is met. The criteria set by the specific venture capitalist can also include significant road traveled down the FDA pipeline for drugs, delivery vehicles, and medical devices, as well as special situations such as putting money behind solving world problems, key technologies, and long-term payouts such as raising nuts in California.

"Family offices and Private Equity may kick in when there is sufficient cash flow, or it is a favorite project of the family," according to Gary Domoracki, managing director and head of the Boston office for Stifel. These scenarios are a guide based on what I have seen in the marketplace.

SAMPLE MOCK DRAFT | Chart 3.1

LOVE IT ICE CREAM, LLC

SUMMARY OF PROPOSED TERMS FOR CONVERTIBLE UNSECURED 6.5% NOTE 2019

The following is sample and mock summary of proposed terms. This term sheet is for discussion purposes only and is not binding on the company or the investors, nor is the company or any investor obligated to consummate the financing note or purchase agreement.

This summary does not purport to be complete and is not qualified in its entirety by the complete note purchase agreement. Investors are urged to read the entire note purchase agreement and contact the company with questions.

The Company: Love It Ice Cream (the "Company") 1000 Moo Way, Hayride, Vermont 10000

Securities Offered: Up to $1,550,000 of the Company's 6.5% Convertible Unsecured Notes (the "Notes"), due 24 months from the date of first issuance of any Note in the Offering, subject to the "Discount Rate" set forth below (this "Offering"). The Company reserves the right to increase the size of the Offering in its sole discretion.

Term of Offering: The Notes shall be offered directly by the Company via a rolling closing until the total aggregate number of Notes are sold, unless such aggregate amount is further increased by the Company in its sole discretion. The Note Purchase Agreement (including investor questionnaires) shall be processed through Upstanding Lawyers LLP counsel to the Company, and is subject to acceptance by the Company. If the Note Purchase Agreement is not so accepted, such investor's funds shall be returned to him, her, or it, without interest or any deduction of any kind.

Maturity Date: Twenty-four (24) months from the date of first issuance of any Notes (the "Maturity Date"), provided that the Notes have not been converted into securities of the Company as provided below.

Interest: Simple interest will accrue on each Note at a rate of 7.0% per annum from the date of issuance of such Note, payable on the date the unpaid principal amount of the Note becomes due and payable, whether at the Maturity Date or earlier by declaration, acceleration or otherwise.

Prepayment: All or any portion of the Notes may be prepaid by the Company only with the prior written consent of investors holding a majority in interest of the aggregate principal number of Notes (the "Majority Note Holders").

If an Equity Financing has not occurred and the Company elects to consummate a Corporate Transaction prior to the Maturity Date, at the election of the Majority Note Holders, then (i) all outstanding principal and unpaid accrued interest due on such Note shall be converted into that number of Conversion Units (as defined in the Note Purchase Agreement) equal to the quotient obtained by dividing the outstanding principal and unpaid accrued interest on a Note to be converted, or portion thereof, on the date of conversion, by the Conversion Price (as defined below); or (ii) the holder shall be paid an amount equal to all outstanding principal and accrued and unpaid interest. "**Corporate Transaction**" shall mean (i) the closing of the sale, transfer or other disposition of all or substantially all of the Company's assets, (ii) the consummation of the merger or consolidation of the Company with or into another entity (except a merger or consolidation in which the holders of the membership interests of the Company immediately prior to such merger or consolidation continue to hold at least 50% of the voting power of the membership interests of the Company or the surviving or acquiring entity), (iii) the closing of the transfer (whether by merger, consolidation or otherwise), in one transaction or a series of related transactions, to a person or group of affiliated persons (other than an underwriter of the Company's securities), of the Company's securities if, after such closing, such person or group of affiliated persons would hold 50% or more of the outstanding membership interests of the Company (or the surviving or acquiring entity) or (iv) a liquidation, dissolution or winding up of the Company; provided, however, that a transaction shall not constitute a Corporate Transaction if its sole purpose is to change the state of the Company's organization or to create a holding company that will be owned in substantially the same proportions by the persons who held the Company's securities immediately prior to such transaction.

Eligible Investors: This Offering is only being made to "accredited investors" as defined by the Securities Act of 1933, as amended (the "Act").

Mandatory Conversion: If, after the date of original issuance of the Notes and prior to the Maturity Date, the Company issues and sells (whether at one closing or a series of closings) equity securities in the Company (the "Equity Securities") resulting in gross proceeds to the Company prior to the Maturity Date of a minimum amount of at least $1,000,000 (excluding the aggregate amount of debt securities converted into Equity Securities upon conversion of the Notes) (the "Next Equity Financing"), then on the first date prior to the Maturity Date on which such minimum gross proceeds have been received by the Company, the entire outstanding principal amount of the Notes, plus all accrued and unpaid interest thereon, shall be converted automatically into Conversion Units on the same terms and conditions (adjusted for the Conversion Price) as the other investors that purchased the Equity Securities in the Next Equity Financing.

Conversion Price: The conversion price (the "Conversion Price") at which the Notes will convert into Conversion Units shall be:

- (i) with respect to a conversion pursuant to a Next Equity Financing, the lower of (A) the product of (x) the applicable Discount Rate (as defined below) and (y) the price paid per unit for Equity Securities by the investors in the Next Equity Financing or (B) the quotient resulting from dividing (x) $7,000,000 by (y) the number of outstanding Common Units of the Company immediately prior to the closing of the Next Equity Financing (assuming conversion of all securities convertible into Common Units, exercise of all outstanding options and warrants to purchase Common Units and including the units reserved or authorized for issuance under the Company's existing equity incentive plan but excluding, for this purpose, the conversion contemplated by Section 2.2 of the Note Purchase Agreement and the conversion of any other convertible promissory notes, SAFEs or similar instruments); and

- (ii) with respect to a conversion pursuant to a Corporate Transaction, the quotient resulting from dividing (x) $7,000,000 by (y) the number of outstanding Common Units of the Company immediately prior to the closing of the Corporate Transaction (assuming conversion of all securities convertible into Common Units, exercise of all outstanding options and warrants to purchase Common Units, but excluding, for this purpose, units available for grant under the Company's equity incentive plan, the conversion contemplated by Section 2.2 of the Note Purchase Agreement and the conversion of any other convertible promissory notes, SAFEs or similar instruments).

"Discount Rate" shall mean: Conversion Explanation:

Based on the Company's current capitalization, if the pre-money valuation of the Next Equity Financing is greater than $7,000,000, then every Common Unit issued upon conversion of the Notes will be calculated at $7,000/unit ($7,000,000/1,000 (total units outstanding today)).* Assuming the foregoing, all of the Notes ($1,500,000 aggregate principal amount) would convert into 217 Common Units (1,550,000/7,000). The total principal amount of the Notes would then constitute a 17.9%** ownership stake in the Company (217/1215).

* This percentage may be lower because the denominator in this formula will increase based on the Next Equity Financing so the ownership percentage may correspondingly decrease.

** If the Company issues more equity to employees before the Next Equity Financing, each Note investor's individual ownership percentage would also decrease as a result. This ownership percentage may also decrease as the Company grows if the Company grants additional stock and/or stock option-based incentives to employees in order to meet Company goals and objectives.

Repayment: If the Notes have not yet been automatically converted upon a Next Equity Financing as of the Maturity Date, the entire outstanding principal amount of, and accrued and

Investment Amount	Applicable Discount
$25,000.00 - $49,999.99	5% discount to the price of the Equity Securities
$50,000.00 - $99,999.99	10% discount to the price of the Equity Securities
$100,000.00 and above	15% discount to the price of the Equity Securities
5% additional discount to the above for Notes issued on or prior to June 1, 2020 (the "**Early Incentive Date**"). The Company has the sole right to extend the Early Incentive Date in its discretion.	

unpaid interest on, the Notes shall become due and payable on demand by the Majority Note Holders.

Amendment: The Note Purchase Agreement and the terms of the Notes may be amended upon the written consent of the Company and the Majority Note Holders; provided that, Section 3.2 of the Note Purchase

Agreement may be amended solely with the written consent of the Company. Notwithstanding the foregoing, the Company may extend the Early Incentive Date without the consent of any investor.

Resale Restrictions: The Notes are not registered under the Act or under any state's securities laws, and may not be sold, hypothecated or otherwise transferred in the absence of an effective registration statement under the Act relating thereto or an opinion of counsel satisfactory to the Company that such registration is not required. The Company undertakes no obligation to affect any such registration.

Representations and Warranties by Investors: Each investor will make customary representations

and warranties regarding its status as an "accredited investor" within the meaning of the Securities Act of 1933, and its knowledge and understanding of the risk factors related to investment in the Company.

Expenses: Each party will bear its own costs and expenses in connection with the negotiation and completion of the transactions contemplated hereby and all related documents.

Confidentiality: This overview and any related correspondence is to be held in strict confidence and is not to be disclosed to any party (other than counsel to, and the accountants of, the parties), without the prior written consent of the Company. We will deal with confidentiality agreements in greater detail below.

Private Equity and Family Office Investments of Lower and Mid-Market: Cash Positive Companies with an EBITDA above $3 Million

The above is an example of an early-stage type of venture agreement. I have invested, disrupted, and accelerated in early-stage seed rounds as well as series A rounds and many more diversified through venture and private equity/family office deals.

As you climb the ladder with increased profitability and value, it becomes a different ball game. Some folks say, "Dave, how the hell does the discussion of private equity investments come into a disruption and acceleration book?" For those that ask, I will say that disruption and acceleration come in many forms. Just because a company is mature doesn't mean that they should cease disruption; and certainly, these companies need to accelerate growth and earnings. That is why it is getting a mention here. There are also those folks that say they love innovation, but we do it in a framework where there is less risk and assurance that we don't lose money.

As an example, an investor would like the preferred equity arrangements of an 18 percent guaranteed return on their money as well as a piece of the equity with targets of multiple two to five times within three years. Then again, who wouldn't? I have seen deals like this offered to get companies to a higher level of acceleration with additional plant capacity.

I have seen pure debt instruments or mezzanine financing on deals like this as well with high-interest levels. Mezzanine financing is a hybrid of debt and equity financing that gives the lender the right to convert to an equity interest in the company in case of default. This situation generally happens after venture capital companies and other senior lenders get paid. And yes, I have seen deals to raise money for new venture funds that will invest in disruptive growth categories.

Also, I have completed private equity and family office deals that have been less lucrative than this. Still, I usually had skin in the game, a piece of equity or convertible equity, which I refer to as "a piece of the rock" with management or board involvement. There's a tendency for people to behave differently when they have a vested interest in the game and ownership. I am a believer in restricted stock awards that pay stock instead of cash. This method is a better way for all parties than straight cash compensation. Profit sharing and milestone bonuses are incentives as well.

Funds themselves are ventures. The minimum size of a more significant type of venture fund is about $250 to $300 million. I have seen funds less than this, but to get serious players behind you, that's the size they're looking for as an investment. Venture funds are great scalable enterprises. I have worked with venture capital groups in scaling their business by increasing their fund size along with a selection of targets and target segments. All of these types of ventures require different forms of legal paperwork.

Intellectual Property

IP needs to be protected. Based on the circumstances, you can protect your new and novel art, as the lawyers call your real difference, with a provisional patent, patent-pending, full patent, or trademark filing. You can also choose not to file a patent and operate with a trade secret. These items need to be flushed out with key stakeholders and exceptional legal advice. This process is incredibly material and vital. You can find free patent information on the US Patent and Trademark Office website. When you have a new or novel idea, consult an experienced attorney such as Doug Kline and Goodwin Procter's team or Bassam "Sam" Ibrahim and his team at Buchanan Ingersoll & Rooney. You can also consult the affiliated resources of your organization, company, university, or school. Ensure that an experienced attorney reviews everything. I am not an attorney, and it is best to consult with one. Companies and people are always looking to steal a good invention. Protection is exceedingly essential.

To save you money on legal fees, here are some items that should get you thinking and assist you in getting organized before discussing your idea with an attorney. Your attorneys may ask other questions, but these questions are a great start:

- Who are the inventors?
- What is the title and description of the invention?
- What is the closest known prior work? You may want to attach any publications known.
- What are the benefits of this invention, and what problems does it solve?
- How is it different than prior approaches, and how does the invention work?
- Do you have diagrams or schematics?
- What are the preferred dimensions, operating parameters?
- What are the flowcharts?
- What are the optional processes?
- Do you have any system diagrams? Architecture?
- What environment does this invention operate in, and what people interact with the invention? What are their roles?
- Describe previous technologies or components that are modified in this specific instance.
- When did you first think of this?
- Are there any records to substantiate your thoughts in terms of a date?
- Did you disclose your idea to anyone? Was there any confidentiality involved? What date? Is there any written evidence?
- Has there been any experimental work done, and when do you plan to go forward with the invention?
- Who observed this process?
- When, if at all, did you make a written description of your invention?
- List any papers, abstracts, etc. describing the published or unpublished submission, including journals or the estimated date of publication.
- Have you made an oral presentation, slide show, or poster? For whom and date?
- Give details of any commercial use or offers to sell this invention.
- Loose Lips Sink Ships! You may forfeit your exclusive rights upon certain publications.
- Do you have any printed publications or drafts set up?
- You will need to show commercial potential and an assessment of the commercial potential and any test market or current commercial use.

The Inverse of Careful Intellectual Property Protocol

A company I once advised released novel and new art before getting protection. They let their invention out of the bag to potential partners and customers. There was a feeding frenzy of customers and competitors looking to file patents based on the concepts proposed. Your IP must be protected so it's not stolen.

Confidentiality Agreements

All parties involved with discussions revolving around confidential information, numbers, and ideas, regardless of the size of the deal, should have a confidentiality agreement in place. The document does not absolutely protect you, but it is a start. Further, if there are scientists that could crack your code, confidentiality may not be enough. It's high-stakes gamesmanship at times. Attorneys should help you navigate through this maze.

A confidentiality agreement can be two ways, for mutual party disclosure, or one way. In employment situations, it's generally one way in that the company is disclosing to the employee and the employee agrees to keep it in confidence. In a potential venture deal, it may be two ways to protect both parties, as both parties may be sharing confidential information for possible synergistic purposes.

AGREEMENT EXAMPLE | Chart 3.2

This Confidentiality and Non-Disclosure Agreement ("Agreement") is entered into as of January 30, 2020 by and between Love It Ice Cream LLC, 1000 Moo Way, Hayride, VT 10000 ("LOVE IT") and Great Taste Dairy LLC ("GTD"), of 2000 Less Filling Drive, Great Taste, NY 20000. All references in this agreement to LOVE IT shall also be deemed to include any subsidiaries of LOVE IT, all its affiliates and all entities under substantially common ownership. All references in this agreement to GTD shall also be deemed to include all subsidiaries of GTD and all of its affiliates including all entities under substantially common ownership.

The Parties desire to enter into preliminary discussions in a formal supply agreement and share confidential and proprietary trade secrets, and other confidential information.

in connection with these discussions, LOVE IT and GTD will each be disclosing certain of their respective "Confidential Information" (as defined below) to the other Party. The Party making any such disclosure is hereafter referred to, in such capacity, as the "Disclosing Party" and the Party receiving any such disclosure of Confidential Information is referred to in such capacity as the "Receiving Party"). LOVE IT and GTD are sometimes referred to herein as a "Party" or collectively as the "Parties". It is a condition to the Parties discussing the Proposed Transaction that the Parties enter into this Agreement.

1. **Definitions**. For purposes of this Agreement, the following terms shall have the definitions described below.

  a. **"Confidential Information"** shall mean all information of a Disclosing Party disclosed to a Receiving Party in connection with the Proposed Transaction, including without limitation all product concepts, designs, plans, prototypes, specifications, product samples, business plans and strategies, marketing plans and strategies, customer and supplier lists, pricing of the Disclosing Party's products and proposed products, research, data, discoveries, developments, inventions, know-how, reports, memoranda and correspondence. Confidential Information disclosed in writing shall be clearly marked as "Confidential" when disclosed. When Confidential Information is disclosed in a manner other than in writing, it shall be summarized and reduced to written form,

marked "Confidential" and transmitted to the Receiving Party within fourteen (14) business days of the initial disclosure. Confidential Information shall not include (i) information that is or becomes part of the public domain, (ii) information that is required to be disclosed by the Receiving Party pursuant to a subpoena or court order, or pursuant to a requirement of a governmental agency or law of the United States of America or state thereof or any governmental or political subdivision thereof, (iii) information that was previously known by the Receiving Party or becomes known by the Receiving Party without violation of any confidentiality obligation, (iv) generic industry information or knowledge that the Receiving Party would have learned in the ordinary course of its business, or (v) information independently developed by the Receiving Party without use of the Confidential Information of the Disclosing Party; provided, however, that the Parties shall take all reasonable steps to prohibit disclosure pursuant to subsection (ii) above.

  b. **"Person"** shall mean any individual, university, corporation, partnership, joint venture, association, joint-stock company, or other entity.

2. **Protection and Non-Disclosure of Confidential Information**. Each Party, in its capacity as a Disclosing Party, agrees that it and its employees will not disclose or communicate in any way, any Confidential Information of the Disclosing Party to any Person other than Persons to whom the owner of said Confidential Information has agreed to permit disclosure of the Confidential Information in advance and in writing. The Receiving Party may disclose Confidential Information to its employees on a need-to-know basis, provided that all such employees are bound by written agreements with the Disclosing Party to maintain the confidentiality of all Confidential Information of the Disclosing Party and its franchisees to which they have access. The Parties hereto will take any and all steps, actions and precautions necessary to ensure that no Confidential Information is disclosed or communicated in any way to any Person other than pursuant to the terms of this Agreement. LOVE IT agrees that it will cause all of its affiliates referenced in the introductory paragraph to this agreement to comply with the terms hereof, and GTD agrees that it will cause all of its affiliates referenced in the introductory paragraph to this agreement to comply with the terms hereof, and each Party shall be responsible for the actions of such Party's affiliates.

3. **Use of the Confidential Information**. Each Party, as a Receiving Party, agrees that it and its employees shall maintain the Confidential Information of the Disclosing Party in confidence and not use any Confidential Information of the Disclosing Party for any purpose other than for evaluating the Proposed Transaction or as agreed upon in writing by the Parties.

4. **Confidential Relationship**. The Parties acknowledge and agree that the disclosure of Confidential Information between the Parties creates a relationship of confidence and trust between the Parties. Upon the request of a Disclosing Party, the Receiving Party and its employees shall immediately cease and desist from the use of any Confidential Information and immediately provide the Disclosing Party with all copies or embodiments, in whatever form, of any and all Confidential Information in its possession or control.

5. **Other Agreements**. Each of the Parties acknowledges and agrees that they are Party to various other agreements, some of which contain obligations regarding confidential information. The Parties intend such other agreements to survive and to continue to govern all disclosures of Confidential Information that do not relate to the Proposed Transaction, but the Parties desire this Agreement to supersede and control all such other agreements with respect to the "Confidential

Information" relating to the Proposed Transaction.

6. **Miscellaneous**. This Agreement shall be governed by and construed in accordance with the laws of the Commonwealth of Massachusetts. This Agreement sets forth the entire understanding between the Parties and supersedes all prior agreements and understandings between the Parties hereto, whether written or oral, with respect to the subject matter hereof. This Agreement may be executed in one or more counterparts, each of which shall be deemed an original, but which together shall constitute one and the same instrument.

7. **Term and Termination**. All terms and provisions of this Agreement shall terminate one year from the date first set forth above; provided, however, that the Parties may request an extension of the term of this Agreement (which consent shall not be unreasonably withheld) if, at the time, disclosure of Confidential Information would be injurious to either Party.

8. **Remedies**. Each Receiving Party acknowledge and agree that any breach or attempted breach of any provision of this Agreement will cause irreparable damage to the Disclosing Party suffering

as a result of the breach and, accordingly, the Parties hereto agree that the breached Party shall be entitled, as a matter of right, to a temporary restraining order, and a temporary, preliminary and permanent injunction out of any court of competent jurisdiction restraining and enjoining any such breach, threatened breach or further breach of this Agreement by breaching Party; such right to any injunction, however, shall be cumulative and in addition to whatever other remedies the breached Party may have at law or in equity.

9. **Invalid Provisions**. If any provision of this Agreement is held to be illegal, invalid, or unenforceable under present or future laws effective during the term hereof, such provisions shall be fully severable and this Agreement shall be construed and enforced as if such illegal, invalid, or unenforceable provision hereof shall remain in full force and effect and shall not be affected by the illegal, invalid or unenforceable provision or by its severance here from.

IN WITNESS WHEREOF, the Parties hereto have executed this Agreement as of the date and year first above written.

LOVE IT ICE CREAM LLC

By: _____

Name: Shawna Miller

Title: President & C.E.O.

GREAT TASTE DAIRY LLC

By: _____

Name: William Johnson

Title: Partner

Trusted Advisors Network, LLC

The upcoming chapters of 4, 5, 6, and 7 describe and explain concepts developed by Trusted Advisors Network, LLC. Trusted Advisors has built tools and resources that have been used with hundreds of clients, helping those clients improve and grow their businesses and organizations through business solutions such as strategic planning, leadership, management, sales development, process improvement, customer loyalty, and professional coaching. The concepts that you will be exposed to in the next four chapters have been created and have evolved as proven business models and practices from the last forty years.

Trusted Advisors has a network of 220 plus consultants and coaches that we support who have access to our tools and resources to support their clients' work. David Radlo is part of our network of highly experienced consultants. Our consultants and coaches have been vetted, trained and contractually have the right to use Trusted Advisors tools and resources.

www.trustedadvisorsnetworkllc.com

Based on David's background and experience, Trusted Advisors has given David Radlo and his company Achievemost express permission to use these concepts as part of this published book. We hope you find great value in David's book and the concepts he has created and chosen to share.

www.achievemost.com

SECTION 3

OPERATIONAL EXCELLENCE:

Align Strategy, People, Processes, And Sustainability To Drive Customer Excellence

OPERATIONAL EXCELLENCE | Chart A

Loyal External Customer

Points of Connection

Internal Customer Satisfaction

System Improvement

Process | Teams | Structures

People Development

Leadership | Attitudes Behaviors

Strategic Planning

Vision | Mission | Values

BASIC FOUNDATION

Business Philosophy   Core Values & Principles

VISION

What the organization will dare to achieve in the next 5 to 15 years

EXTERNAL ASSESSMENT

Market segments & opportunities

Competitive analysis

Trend analysis

INTERNAL APPRAISAL

Structure & function

Resources

Strengths, limitations, opportunities, and threats

MISSION

What the Organization will Achieve Within the Next 12-18 Months

CRITICAL GOALS CATEGORIES

Define 3 or 4 Areas that will enable your organization to meet the vision and mission

These are General Categories and Not Specific Goals

GOALS

Create Smart Goals to Drive the Organization and Mission

ACTION STEPS

Defines the Actions that Must be accomplished to meet your goals

MARKET PLAN

Product offerings

Segment strategies

Market communications

Sales support

SALES PLAN

Territory strategies

Key account strategies

Personal development

BUDGETING

Sales volume   Financial profit and loss

Costs   Cash flow statements

Expenses   Extra reports: Daily cash and AR/AP reports

Capital requirements

CHAPTER FOUR

PRINCIPLE IV: Prepare a Versatile Strategic Business Plan with the Anticipation of Modifications.

Strategic planning will walk you through every step necessary to create and implement a practical and effective organizational plan. The basic foundation will be your business philosophy. What are your core values and principles? Begin with the end in mind. What is your vision for the next five to fifteen years? Your vision will serve as a source of motivation and as a guide in the decisions you will make as you move forward. *Chart 4.1 on page 58* is an outline of the different items found in a strategic business plan.

Basic Foundation and Business Philosophy

Your business philosophy establishes the ground rules and gets the most crucial part of your plan in place. As stakeholders, all members need to create the foundation for the vision statement. Focus on the organization's reason for being in business and how those reasons positively impact the customer. When you consider short- and long-term objectives, identify all future payoffs and return on investment to your organization.

Vision

A compelling vision statement is a statement that is written simply in as few words as possible. It should be big and bold while having an "aha" effect. Everyone must be involved in the process of creating it. Your vision statement should come from the heart, and it's not about the money. It should be higher than a traditional goal. Revisit your vision statement often to stay focused on the purpose of your work.

The vision sets the stage for what the organization aspires to become, create, and achieve. The vision statement should be timeless, evoke energy, and drive action. The vision's time frame should range from five to fifteen years unless the vision is multigenerational; in that case, it could range from fifty to a hundred years or more.

You need to start thinking about the following:

- Are you interested in fast, aggressive growth versus slow, controlled growth? What is the scope you want to become? (Your answers will assist you to plan for staffing and financing.)

- What size organization do you want to become? $100,000, $1,000,000, $50,000,000, $100,000,000, $1,000,000,000 in revenue?
- Will your locations/operations primarily be local, statewide, regional, national, or international?
- Will you be singular or multidivisional?
- Do you want to grow through organic growth, mergers and acquisitions, franchising, licensing, or other ways unique to your industry?
- What legacy do you want your organization to be known for? Does this matter?

It is important that consensus and buy-in occur with the vision.

Values

Your values help develop the internal parameters for the culture and all contributors' behaviors throughout the entire organization. Values are statements that should be nonnegotiable. People need to be able to comply with your values. Lack of adherence to values must have consequences.

If your participants talk about vendors as partners, you may want to ask how they select and keep vendors. Are they talking about this relationship as a partnership, but in practice going for the low-cost provider? Does integrity matter? Does this behavior match the values? If not, what do they need to do about the issue to remedy this situation?

There must also be an agreement on how to share the values with the organization. Consider the following questions: How will your participants communicate their values? What manner will they teach the values to every participant and team member? What processes will be put in place to hold the leadership accountable for embodying the values daily and in their decision-making process? How will the issue be remedied if someone or a group is not embodying the values?

Mission Statement

A mission statement is a broad statement that identifies the scope of the business. It addresses how your organization will realize the vision. It defines what the organization will do and by implication what it will not do. The mission defines the boundaries of the future organization. Your mission usually defines a shorter time frame of eighteen months. There could be a long-term mission based on the longevity of the business and vision that could multigenerational.

As a general rule, the mission should be transparent, so all contributors and team members align their activities to achieve it. There are situations, however, where an essential element or goal in the mission must be for the planning team's eyes only. The participants need to decide what exactly is to be communicated, how frequently, when, and to whom.

Include the following functions:

- Indicate a change in outcomes such as to increase, decrease, prevent, eliminate, promote, or to become something
- Identify a challenge or condition to be improved
- Identify an opportunity to be maximized

As an example, an organization may have a vision for a world free of Ebola. In that case, the organization's mission might be stated as: We will conduct research aimed at defining a vaccine to prevent people from contracting Ebola that can be easily distributed and administered around the world.

You can finalize the mission statement outside of the planning meeting. Still, it's most desirable for the final wording to be created by the organization as a whole, not by the facilitator. This method creates a higher level of buy-in and communication. Communicating the mission statement is just as important as creating it. Facilitate a discussion about how your organization communicates your mission.

Goals

Goals will enable your organization to meet your vision and mission. Choose three or four general categories for these goals. John Doerr, author of the *New York Times* best seller *Measure What Matters*, developed a simple goal formula:

I/WE WILL _____ (GOAL) AS MEASURED BY _____ (THIS SET OF KEY RESULTS).

The goal will describe what you will achieve, how you will measure it, and how you will track the results. If your goal is to excite your customers, what will your results be? How will you measure the outcome, their level of excitement? What data will you review? Also, set a time frame for data measurement.

From this point, create SMART Goals. A SMART Goal is Specific, Measurable, Attainable, Relevant, and Timely. This type of goal is more targeted to your organization's mission. Saying you want to increase sales may be a good goal, but it is not specific. Stating you intend to increase sales by 20 percent in the second quarter is more concrete. Specifically, you have to know what you are aiming for so you can take the action required to get there.

External Assessment

To determine where you want your organization to go, you must first conduct an organizational assessment. The data you collect will allow you to create an executable plan for future growth. You will need to assess the market segments or target markets for your product or service. This part of the assessment will help you to define segments by customer population, needs, and potential sales opportunities. Define your ideal customer and understand your ideal customers' demographics.

The market segment assessment will also allow you to assess the competition in your space. A competitive analysis is needed to learn how well your organization is designed for competitive performance. By targeting a specific group of customers, you can tailor your product or service. This will allow you to enhance your competitive edge.

Market Segments and Opportunities: Complete an external assessment using your organization's preexisting internal knowledge of markets, competition, etc. However, if you have done formalized research in these areas, you should use that information as well. It's not necessary to focus on data that is statistically significant about a specific percentage of market share. The point is to create an understanding of the room for growth in your existing and potential markets.

Product/Service Competitive Analysis: Participants should rate themselves and create action steps for improvement if needed. Compare product factors with key competitors. Find out how your organization's products or services compare to your competition.

Organizational Competitive Analysis: Compare your organization with your key competitors. Identify the factors of strength on your part and weaknesses of your competitors that you can exploit. Does your organization plan your future based on what your competition is doing? Or, do you have a unique strategy regardless of what your competition is doing? You can complete this information with your organization's internal knowledge, but formal research may be warranted. It would help if you also considered how to stay up to date as time progresses.

Finally, complete a trend analysis to understand the broader economic, social, political, global, and cultural issues that exist in your markets. This assessment will allow your team to know how to respond to the positive or negative effects of the emerging trends.

The assessment is a growth and competition exercise. Where do you fit? What fast-growing segments of large markets do you want to explore organically? Are there ripe add-ons that are acquisition targets making up pipeline targets? There is more than one way to grow. If you are in a mature business, but competitors or similar companies located in different geographies want to exit, is this an opportunity for growth?

The Importance of Competitive Analysis (Trusted Advisors)

Is Your Competition Your Secret to Success?

Often the key to success in any business relates to how you stack up against the competition. Although it might sound strange, your competition is what can drive production, development, and better service. You have to study your competition. It's called competitive analysis, and it's one of the most important tasks you can do as a business owner.

Complacency can be the downfall of your organization. When you stop innovating, you open the door to your competition, even if you think you don't have any at the time. Have you ever seen a game where a competitor started celebrating before they won? Then, in the final seconds, the opponent pulls ahead to win because they were more focused on their performance? To succeed in the game of business, you must continually adapt, innovate, and make improvements to have a spot in the race.

As you study your competition, push yourself to find ways to stand out in the market. You have to find ways to become the leader in your industry. Through this process, your self-awareness will increase. You should always be assessing your company's strengths and weaknesses. This process will allow you to create more value and improved service for your customers. To be a leader in the market, you must continually show your customers why they should choose your company over the competition. You must differentiate your offerings so that you create tremendous value for them.

In the process, you will gain knowledge about your customers, market, and emerging trends. The new patterns that emerge will allow you to develop and promote your products and services within that market. To build a profitable business, focus your efforts on conquering a smaller segment of the market. By narrowing your niche, you can develop a competitive edge that deters further competition.

Observations of your competition's management and business practices can lead to significant learning. You will see their use of resources and management styles. This information can help you to adopt new methods that will work best for your company.

In some cases, studying the competition can lead to an unexpected partnership. Sometimes the best way to compete with someone is to join forces. You can create an alliance with another business in your field to exchange technology, knowledge, resources, tools, and market. The collaboration is an opportunity to cross-promote each other's products.[5]

How to Complete a Competitive Analysis

Step 1: Identify your current and potential competition. Group all of your competitors by the degree to which they contend for the buyer's dollar, or group competitors according to their various competitive strategies, so you understand what motivates them.

Step 2: Once you have identified your competitors, take the time to analyze them. Look at their business strategies. Pay attention to their strengths and weaknesses. Their strengths can serve as a guide to how you should do business. Their weaknesses can show you where the competition is most vulnerable and help you find ways to exploit that to your benefit.

The strength and weakness evaluation should cover four areas:

1. The reasons behind successful as well as unsuccessful firms
2. Prime customer motivators (Why did the customer choose them?)
3. Major component costs
4. Industry mobility barriers

Step 3: Create a competitive strengths grid. This grid will include key assets and skills in a particular area, along with a notation of "weakness" and "strength" for each competitor. The five areas should include product, distribution, pricing, promotion, and advertising.[6]

Once you've finished collecting the data for the competitive analysis, you want to pay attention to several areas as you comb through your findings.

Market Gaps: Identify unserved or underserved gaps in the market. A competitor map may reveal that most competitors in the local area charge premium prices for higher-quality products, while the bargain segment of the market remains underserved.

Product Development: You will learn what your competition has in development, and you'll also be able to see ways they are improving their product or service. Knowing the direction competitors plan to take for their product lines can help a company develop products that trump competitors in terms of price, functionality, or quality.

Market Trends: Spotting new market trends is essential. Your competitive analysis will not only identify these trends but develop ways to exploit them.

Marketing Practices: It's not enough to provide a great product or give exceptional customer service. It would be best if you studied your competition's marketing strategies. Find out how they're branding themselves as a company as well as their products. What channels do they use? How much money are they spending? You also want to pay attention to what customers think of your competitors. What consumers believe they are buying can be more important than what they are actually buying, and it is advantageous to know what consumers think about your competitors' brands.

With these tips for creating a competitive analysis, you will be better able to gauge what your competition is doing and determine how to do it better.[7]

Internal Appraisal

An internal appraisal is required to determine what resources are needed to achieve your goals. Complete this part of your plan after you define what your critical success factors are. You should address your organization's structure with the markets you serve and with your vision and values. Gain an understanding of your strengths and limitations, as well as your opportunities and threats. Your organization's processes should be aligned to address all critical success factors. Once you identify concerns, formulate actionable ideas to address the potential issues.

Structure and Function: The structure and function section's purpose is to discover processes and structural advantages that your organization should capitalize on or improve. This is one area where participants might want to rush to judgment. You might see individual items or low-hanging fruit, and you will want to attack quickly. To obtain the best outcome, stick with the process. Create a mission next, so you create goals and key results that are focused on the best priorities. Your mission will determine the alignment of your opportunities and will help the organization identify the right priorities. You may want to create an idea parking lot to record items participants wish to resolve for future conversations. Use your time together to make sure someone is accountable for all the listed ideas. Have a follow-up session for accountability for the completion of the tasks.

Resources: The resources section of your assessment will uncover specific resources the organization needs, if any, to achieve the organization's goals.

Strengths, Limitations, Opportunities, and Threats: These questions will help you consider your organization's readiness to improve. A SLOT analysis is an excellent tool to identify the organization's current strengths, limitations, opportunities, and threats. Facilitating this tool allows the organization to see at a glance where they stand concerning their perceived strengths, limitations, opportunities, and threats for and to the organization.

SLOT Analysis

SLOT is an acronym that stands for the internal Strengths and Limitations of an organization and the external potential Opportunities and Threats that currently exist. A SLOT analysis helps an organization to evaluate itself, for better or worse, by providing a better understanding of what it does well and where it should improve. A SLOT analysis will help an organization size up the competitive landscape and provide insights into the constant changes in their marketplace. It provides a framework to choose from many options. Its simplicity develops a strategy by matching the organization's strengths and limitations with its opportunities and threats.

In our frame of reference, a SLOT analysis can be viewed as a simple framework for generating strategic alternatives from the analysis of a business situation. It applies to the corporate level, to a business unit, and a personal level. Used in the business context, it helps carve a sustainable niche in your market. Used in a personal context, it enables you to develop your career in a way that takes the best advantage of your talents, abilities, and opportunities.

Because a SLOT analysis concentrates on the issues that potentially have the most impact on a business, it is useful when a limited amount of time is available to address a complex situation. The amount of input and quality of the input determines the quality of the SLOT analysis. If you develop a SLOT analysis with only one person, the CEO, for example, it is more likely the information will differ from the results than if the senior leadership team had involvement. Also, you would probably get a different outcome if you surveyed customers and interviewed contributors and team members. For our purposes, when used in conjunction with a strategic planning process, the strategic planning team should have sufficient knowledge to complete the matrix.

The following diagram shows how the SLOT analysis fits into a strategic situation analysis:

STRATEGIC ANALYSIS | Chart 4.2

SITUATION ANALYSIS
Desired Outcome, Goal, or Vision

INTERNAL ANALYSIS

Strengths	Limitations
Offense	Defense

EXTERNAL ANALYSIS

Opportunities	Threats
Offense	Defense

The SLOT matrix is produced by matching specific internal and external factors to create a strategic matrix. The matrix matches Strengths with Opportunities (S/O), Strengths with Threats (S/T), Limitations with Opportunities (L/O), and Limitations with Threats (L/T). These combinations and matrix quadrants provide senior leadership with an organized approach to develop strategies that can:

- Build on their strengths in order to capitalize on opportunities (S/O)
- Strive to use their strengths to minimize competitive threats (S/T)
- Minimize or eliminate perceived limitations while making the most of any new opportunities (L/O)
- Minimize an organization's internal limitations and minimize external threats (L/T)

The beauty of a SLOT analysis is that it can serve as an interpretative filter to reduce the information to a manageable number of key issues. As a generalization, strengths can serve as a foundation for building a competitive advantage, and limitations hinder it. By understanding the four aspects of the SLOT matrix, an organization can better leverage its strengths, overcome its limitations, capitalize on current robust opportunities, and deter potentially devastating threats.

Getting Started: The first step of a SLOT analysis is to develop a definition of the desired end state, i.e., objective, goal, or vision. This end state must be understood and accepted by all participants. After you identify the end state, facilitate a SLOT analysis to focus on the attainment of the vision. Analyze the strengths, limitations, opportunities, and threats.

Internal Strengths: Internal strengths enable your organization to put its best foot forward while achieving its vision. A strength is a resource or a skill that is controlled internally. It allows an organization to meet its market demands and stand firm or above competitors. Examples could include financial resources, marketing, leadership, core competencies, influence, relationships, company culture, company image, structure, key contributors, operational efficiency, brand awareness, exclusive contracts, capabilities, experience, marketing, geographic location, management philosophy, attitudes, innovation, patents, and trade secrets.

Key questions that can be asked to help identify an organization's specific strengths:

- What are your specific advantages?
- What does your organization do well?
- How strong is your organization in the marketplace?
- What is your organization's strong strategic advantage?

- Does your organization's culture produce a positive work advantage?
- What unique resources do you or can you draw upon?
- What are your organizations core competencies?
- What do you do so well that you could create a business model out of just that one competency?
- What do contributors, team members, customers, vendors, suppliers, and the community see as your organization's strengths?

Internal Limitations: Limitations are the weak points found in an organization. Every organization has them. The deficiency of resources, skills, capabilities, and potentialities impact effective performance. Examples of limitations include lack of new products, lack of competitive strength, lack of supply chain robustness, morale, accreditations, processes and systems, management succession, interdepartmental cooperation, managerial abilities, market trends, financial issues, capacity, company culture, company image, operational capacity, operational efficiency, market share, access to natural resources, and key staff that need to be geared up to meet situations.

Key questions that can be asked to help identify your specific limitations:

- What can be improved at your company?
- What does your company do poorly?
- What should be avoided?
- Is your company unable to finance needed technology?
- Do you have an overabundance of debt or cash flow issues?
- Where do you have fewer resources to draw upon than others?
- What are others likely to see as your weaknesses?
- What can you improve?

External Opportunities: Opportunities provide for a robust future. External opportunities are possible lifelines for the future, but they may not be controllable by the organization. They represent significant favorable situations in the organization's business environment. Examples might include new technology, market trends, customers, competitors, competitor's vulnerability, global influences, niche target markets, new markets, significant contracts, business and product development, distribution, production economies, seasonal influences, fashion influences, suppliers, partners, social changes, economic environment, political environment, and the regulatory environment.

Key questions that can be asked to help identify your organization's specific opportunities:

- What favorable market or business circumstances are you currently involved in?
- What are the current market trends? Is your organization positioned to take on those trends?
- Is your organization entering new markets?
- Is your organization's technology advancing?
- What are the good opportunities facing your organization right now?
- What are current changes in technology and markets on both a broad and narrow scale?
- What are potential changes in government policy related to your industry?
- What are potential changes in social patterns, population profiles, and lifestyle changes that impact your product or service, your business?
- How can you turn your strengths to opportunities?

External Threats: External threats are like ticking time bombs. Identify them and take preventive measures immediately. You can identify external threats by observing the competition, market trends, upward or downward growth strategies, bargaining, technological changes, etc. Examples might include customers, competitors, market trends, suppliers, partners, social changes, new technology, economic environment, vital contracts, new services, insurmountable weaknesses, global economy, seasonality, political climate, and the regulatory environment.

Key questions that can be asked to help identify your organization's specific threats:

- What current market obstacles do you face?
- What is your competition doing currently that may be different?
- Are the required specifications for your products or services changing?
- What policies are local and federal lawmakers backing? Do they affect your industry?
- Does your organization have bad debt or cash flow issues?
- What current trends can cause your organization harm?
- What threats do your weaknesses expose your organization to that you are not working on right now?
- What does your organization need to avoid?
- Are the required specifications for your organization's products or services changing?

- Is changing technology threatening your position?
- Can any of your weaknesses seriously threaten your business?
- What could put your organization out of business?

Once you create your SLOT matrix, identify the organization's top three to six Strengths, Limitations, Opportunities, and Threats on the vertical and horizontal axes of the SLOT matrix. After you complete the analysis, the team can develop strategies and goals for the interaction of the quadrants in the SLOT profile. For example, you can leverage the strengths to pursue opportunities and to avoid threats. Senior leaders can be alerted to liabilities to pursue opportunities successfully.

To develop the possible strategies or goals in the inner boxes of the matrix, repeatedly ask and answer the following four questions:

1. How can we use each Strength?
2. How can we stop each Limitation?
3. How can we exploit each Opportunity?
4. How can we defend against each Threat?

Sometimes, by sorting the SLOT analysis into six planning categories, you can create a system that presents a practical way of using internal and external information about an organization. You can delineate short- and long-term priorities and provide an easy way for the senior leadership team to achieve their goals and objectives.

The suggested six categories are:

1. Product – What are we selling?
2. Process – How are we selling and making it?
3. Customer – To whom are we selling it?
4. Distribution – How does it reach the customer?
5. Finance – What are the prices, costs, investments?
6. Administration – How do we manage all of this?

Sorting will make it easier to break the SLOT issues into actionable items that become more quantifiable and measurable. Clarity in strategy works. Fuzzy strategies fail. Most strategies fail because they don't have a clear direction.

Critical Success Factors

Critical Success Factors (CSFs) must pass two tests: they must be individually necessary and together sufficient to achieve the mission.

While CSFs may be considered broad categories, they are specific to your industry and desired markets. The SLOT exercise should address your strengths and limitations.

Here are a few examples of CSFs:

- Maintain Adequate Cash Flow
- Ensure Best of Breed Quality
- Maintain a Competitive Cost Structure
- Ensure Only Motivated, Well-Trained Contributors Exist at Every Level
- Increase Revenue
- Minimize Waste
- Invest in State-of-the-Art Equipment
- Grow Emerging Leaders
- Enhance Research and Development Efforts
- Increase Speed to Market for All Products

When appropriately stated, the CSFs will provide an opportunity to create several intermediate milestones to realize them. For example, a CSF of minimizing waste is a broad category that might then be fulfilled by creating the following intermediate milestones:

- By 6/30/XX, our organization will evaluate our current manufacturing location to determine if the plant can support two new manufacturing lines for product ____ and product ____ estimating an increased revenue opportunity of X million dollars.

- By 3/31/XX, the product development team will interview all ____ suppliers and introduce them to our newly designed product specifications with the goal to create long-term vendor relationships that support revenue for them and an estimated savings of XX.X% to our organization.

- By 9/30/XX, the operations team will conduct, simultaneously, two cycle time reduction processes on the ____ process and the____ process to locate and eliminate bottlenecks while calculating and then reporting the estimated savings to senior leadership.

Here is a generic version:

- By 12/31/XX, our organization will generate X million in revenue and have a business presence in every state east of the Mississippi. We will also have added ____ new products to better serve the ____ market and ____ new services to better serve the ____ and ____ markets.

From this intermediate milestone, the teams and/or individuals will start to create specific GKRs to implement the necessary action steps to achieve the intermediate milestones and, ultimately the CSFs.

The strategic planning team should create somewhere between four and eight CFSs, depending upon the size of the organization, as the optimal amount for focus. As they are completed, new CFSs can be created to keep the progress moving in a positive and fluid direction.

Critical Success Factors Overlay

The next step for the strategic planning team is to take their critical success factors and overlay them onto the appropriate processes within their organization. This exercise will allow them to see where and how their defined critical success factors overlay onto their organization's processes. The spreadsheet is intentionally designed to be detailed and thorough. When done well, participants can physically see the overlapping touchpoints their defined critical success factors have to multiple processes in the organization. The evaluation tool touches on the following areas of an organization.

- Market-Sensing Processes
- Market and Business Intelligence
- New Offering Processes
- Revenue Generation
- Relationship Management Processes
- Accounting and Financial Controls
- Information Management Processes
- Infrastructure
- Business Continuity
- Generating Hardware/Software
- Manufacturing/Assembly
- Human Resources
- Wholesale Operations
- Retail Operations
- Physical Facilities

Execution Plan

Intermediate Milestones:

An organization's mission statement, when succinctly stated, communicates the current direction of the organization. Critical success factors translate the mission and vision into specifics that should be clearly articulated and understood. The intermediate milestones describe what the organization wants to achieve during a specific time frame, thus providing direction for all team members.

State your milestones in paragraph form. The paragraph describes the future state of your organization and reflects an appropriate time frame for completion. The size of your organization and current market conditions may determine the timeline used to create intermediate milestones. For larger organizations, the milestones may have a two- to three-year horizon; for smaller organizations, the horizon may be one year, and in some cases, you may use both. Select a time frame that is most meaningful to you.

Milestones Examples

By 6/30/XX, our unit will recruit, hire, and train 250 frontline manufacturing employees in order to meet the corporation's goal to have the new plant located in _____ production-ready by 12/31/XX.

By 7/15/XX our bank will have expanded by 3 branch locations, specifically located in _____, _____, and _____. We will also have unveiled our updated business and personal mobile banking products, which have estimated revenue of an increase of X.X%

By 12/31/XX, our organization will be a tri-state retail operation by opening new locations in _____ and _____ to better penetrate the _____ and _____ markets.

Goals and Key Results:

The milestones set the stage for starting the Goals and Key Results (GKR) process. Given the milestones, you can then determine the intermediate steps necessary to meet the milestones. For instance, if the milestones are a statement of what the organization wants to accomplish in the next eighteen months, you might decide that quarterly GKRs represent the pace and measurement frequency necessary to meet the milestones. Given that, you can determine the top level GKRs to be accomplished in each quarter.

The GKR process recognizes that the world changes while you make other plans. Therefore, the quarterly GKRs you set now will need to be adjusted as you review the results of the past quarters and set new GKRs for the next quarter.

In the GKR process, most goals are qualitative statements, followed by key result statements that are quantitative. However, in the GKR process, the goal can be a quantitative or qualitative description of what you want to achieve. What makes the GKR concept so powerful is that either a quantitative or qualitative goal will be driven by the key results that will be measured and tracked. This process makes the intangible tangible. The GKRs are the vehicle to which your plan gets implemented. Your team should develop your GKRs for the time frame that is most useful to the organization. However, most organizations use a very manageable window of three months or quarters.

GKRs are stated in the following format: We/I will accomplish _____ (the goal) as measured by _____ (the result).

GKRs might look like the following:

Goal: Delight our customers.

Key Results:

1. Increase customer retention from X% to Y%.

2. Increase our net promoter score from X% to Y%.

3. Increase clicks on our product pages from X to Y.

Every team and individual contributor will have a set of GKRs that support what the organization is seeking to accomplish in a given quarter. I recommend that all GKRs are visible and transparent to every team member throughout your entire organization. It is vital to develop your process, the meetings and measurements, and necessary to set quarterly GKRs and measure how well the results were achieved. In most organizations, results are self-reported by the person who set the GKRs. Person A would state: Here are my goals and critical results I planned for this past quarter. Here are the results I achieved. In preparation for our next quarter, here are my proposed GKRs.

Most organizations using this concept do not use the GKRs as the foundation for contributor performance measurement. In organizations using the GKR process, contributors are encouraged to set results at a relatively high level, thus aiming for high performance. In that case, one might expect that even if 70 percent of the results were achieved, the organization has made substantial progress toward its intermediate milestones.

The GKR process will help you focus and create a pace for your organization to march forward to meet your intermediate milestones. As an example, the theme for the next quarter may be to acquire ten new customers. Based on this theme, you will ask your participants to set GKRs to support the theme of acquiring ten new customers while still focusing on current business. As an example, the product manager may set the following GKRs:

Goal: Package new software features to offer customers.

Key Results:

1. Design new packaging by week one.
2. Create new sales literature by week two.
3. Roll out everything to the sales team by week three.

Other examples you can use with your group to help generate a clear understanding include the following:

Theme: Update the employee handbook.

Goal: Review and update employee benefit section of the handbook (HR Director).

Key Results:

1. Review current benefits and overlap them for accuracy with what is stated in the current handbook by 1/5/XX.
2. Input necessary changes and updates by 1/10/XX.
3. Submit updated benefit section for handbook submission to VP of HR by 1/20/XX.

Theme: Create prospect drip campaigns in the CRM.

Goal: Create ten customer stories to be used as a drip email in our prospect campaigns (Content Editor).

Key Results:

1. Create a ten question survey asking our customer to share their personal story by 9/3/XX.
2. Run the survey on 9/10/XX.
3. Evaluate the results of the survey by 9/15/XX.
4. Take usable stories and migrate them into the designed campaign format by 9/25/XX.
5. Proof and make corrections by 9/27/XX.
6. Email the ten final stories to the CMO by 9/30/XX.

The never-ending quarterly theme and GKR process is a graphic visual you can hand out to show the participants to fuel the organization's ability to achieve the defined CSFs as well as future CSFs.

Marketing the Plan

An individual or a separate department from the primary planning group of participants can write the marketing plan. If this is the case, the drafts of the plan should be presented to the primary planning group to ensure that all intermediate milestones and GKRs are in alignment.

The Sales Plan

An individual or department separate from the main planning process can write the sales plan. If this is the case, the drafts of the plan should be presented to the leading planning group to ensure that all intermediate milestones and GKRs are in alignment.

Follow-Up Tools

As discussed earlier in this process, the more that every team member and contributor understands how their daily activities and productivity impacts the success of the plan, the more committed they will be to contribute to the achievement of your organization's vision positively. As the senior leadership team, it is your job to consistently, frequently, and effectively communicate where the organization stands with its identified goals. The recap, goal summary, and financial worksheets can be essential tools to make communication smooth and seamless.

This section contains a sample strategic planning recap, goal summary, and financial worksheets that I recommend as an effective way to communicate the details of your organization's plan to your contributors and team members.

Critical Success Factors – Process Overlay: This will allow your participants to see where their defined critical success factors overlay onto their organizations' processes. The spreadsheet is intentionally thorough so your participants can see the overlapping touchpoints their defined critical success factors have on multiple processes in the organization.

Strategic Planning Recap Worksheet: Create a one-page document recapping the essence of your plan. As the senior leadership team, you can quickly and easily monitor progress, decide what course corrections to take, and celebrate your accomplishments. It can be a powerful tool to communicate and share information with your team members and contributors.

Goals Summary Worksheet: This provides an easy way to summarize and communicate your vision, mission, values, and your critical success factors while listing the specifics goals needed to make each critical success factor a reality. This worksheet will also help prioritize all the identified goals while communicating the expected completion date and which member of the senior leadership team is championing which goal(s).

Daily Cash: You must understand your organization's financials. It is critical also to monitor your daily cash position. Decisions you make impact your financials daily. It is a valuable exercise to review historical data and forecast financial projections. The success and sustainability happen when you are in a position to make sound financial decisions daily.

Overall Cash Flow Worksheet: This worksheet allows you to review your cash flow for a window of thirty days. As discussed above, historical data and financial forecasting are essential. However, the shorter window in which you manage and control your organization's cash flow will reduce and potentially eliminate financial surprises.

In completing your strategic plan, value proposition, and strategic planning traps, take time to reflect on them for circumstances of change. Also, realize you will often require three times more capital than you think you will need.

On the wall next to my desk, I tore out a page from a *Business Week* magazine from back in the early 2000s. Here are some basic traps you can fall into with strategic planning.

Strategic Plan Traps

1. Failure to recognize and understand events and changing conditions in the competitive environment.

2. Basing strategies on a flawed set of assumptions.

3. Pursuing a one-dimensional strategy that fails to create or sustain a long-term competitive advantage.

4. Diversifying for all of the wrong reasons.

5. Failing to structure and implement mechanisms to ensure the coordination and integration of core processes and essential functions across organizational boundaries.

6. Setting arbitrary and inflexible goals and implementing a system of controls that fails to achieve a balance among culture, rewards, and boundaries.

7. Failing to provide leadership essential to the successful implementation of strategic change.

8. Be sure to get a great attorney that you can trust. Even if you play by the rules, you may be sued for a number of reasons. Legal action is a strategy. Do your best to avoid litigation and regulatory violations. Stay ahead of the game.

Begin with the end in mind when in discussion with investors. They are looking for payback and an exit before they invest. There is a difference between a private equity investor, which is a short-term investor, and a strategic ownership investor, which is a long-term investor. Understand angel investors as well. Angel investors are individuals who provide capital for a business start-up. This arrangement is usually in exchange for convertible debt or ownership equity. Not everyone will be willing to do angel investing.

If you are positioning the company for revenue, it is judged differently than if you are a technical company that is developing IP. Your value may not be consistent with profits and EBITDA. Emerging tech companies or medical device companies base their value from benchmarks and milestones.

Summary

To achieve your objectives, you must clearly articulate your vision, mission, and critical success factors. The better you understand your market and your resources, the better position you will be in to succeed. It's essential to know your strengths and limitations to address them early. Your strategic plan is the foundation and road map to your success. This plan should be revisited often for continuous improvement. To start a strategic plan, have a clear understanding of your cash requirements. Queries will arise about the difference between your cash flow projections and your profit and loss. In new ventures, the focus should be on conserving and maximizing the use of your precious cash resources.

CHAPTER FIVE

PRINCIPLE V: Clearly Understand and Utilize People Resources.

People Research

As a company, you have to have the leadership and the right people focused on the desired result. Results improve when people overcome the automatic pilot of attitudes and beliefs ingrained from childhood. Positive behavior change comes from the improvement of attitude, skills, and knowledge. According to Trusted Advisors, 85 percent of CEOs believe attitude is more important than skills and knowledge (Trusted Advisors).

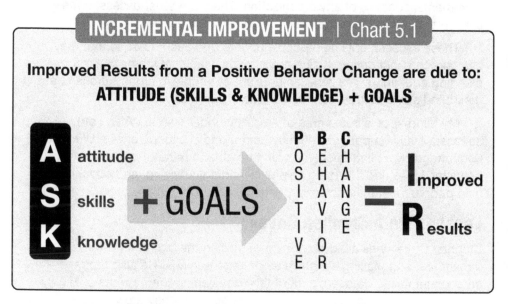

INCREMENTAL IMPROVEMENT | Chart 5.1

Improved Results from a Positive Behavior Change are due to:
ATTITUDE (SKILLS & KNOWLEDGE) + GOALS

A attitude

S skills **+ GOALS** → **POSITIVE BEHAVIOR** **CHANGE** **=** **Improved Results**

K knowledge

Understanding the Driver

I am a big believer in understanding blind spots of people in an organization. An organization can function better by everyone on the management team knowing each other's blind spots and increasing people's self-awareness level. I became a Certified Innermetrix analyst because this tool has become indispensable to run and advise organizations and businesses.

Based on the types of people who are in an organization, there are different programs necessary to improve and create motivation. As part of my board member executive coaching practice at Achievemost, my certification as an Innermetrix analyst has become a crucial part of creating positive change for my clients. In that capacity, for key executives on a team, as well as for personal development, it is suggested that an Innermetrix Advanced Insight Profile (Copyright 2018 Innermetrix Incorporated – All Rights Reserved) that combines the best of three world-class profiles is taken. The Attribute Index measures how you think and make decisions. The Values Index measures your motivational style and drivers, and the DISC Index measures your preferred behavior style. Together, they uncover the natural abilities that you have, what motivates you, and how you prefer to use your talents. This level of awareness identifies your blind spots and allows executives and all people to achieve peak performance. This assessment is integral to alignment in any organization.

Self-awareness and team awareness are crucial to maximizing the incremental success of any organization. There are other assessments available, but I find the Innermetrix Analysis to be the best in this vein.

These assessments help people understand each other so that they can take the best action. It also helps guide executive teams with proper planning and hiring. The assessments assist people in organizations to see their blind spots so they can remedy the challenges.

My blind spot is in the area of empathy under stress. When I am stressed, I lack empathy, and I may get loud to cut to the chase. Without understanding a blind spot, you won't be able to reframe or transform your behavior. I also find this quite helpful in leading, advising, and coaching to help people meet their goals, aspirations, and right action.

Lessons from Stephen Covey

Stephen Covey was a big proponent of putting the big rocks in the bucket first and placing a high value on urgent things. He also focused on accountability. He spent a lot of time developing the 7 Habits of Highly Effective People, and they are worth introspection. They are valuable lessons about people's interactions and management. A copy of these habits is a pillar on my wall.

1. Take responsibility for your own actions and be proactive.

2. Begin with the end in mind. Develop a mission statement based upon values and stated goals and objectives.

3. Prioritize. Put first things first.

4. Seek first to understand before being understood. Develop relationships. Be a mentor, teacher, organizer, and model.

5. Think Win, Win.

6. Synergize as a team and work towards interdependence (from dependence to independence to interdependence).

7. Renewal. Seek to continue to improve your skills and abilities.

Understand Management Traps

Also, on my wall, courtesy of *US News and World Report* circa 2000, are management traps to avoid:

1. Superior attitude, self-centeredness, and not being able to see the impact of their management styles upon others.

2. Rigid and inflexible management styles.

3. Poor communication skills.

4. Micromanaging, unwillingness to delegate, and/or not being able to work through others.

5. Failure to develop subordinates.

6. Inability to deal with an increasingly diverse and aging workforce, and/or lack of sensitivity to cultural issues poised by an expanding global marketplace.

7. Unable to make the leap from managing subordinates to managing managers.

Violate them at your own risk.

Executive Planning: Leadership, Management, and Goal Setting

People are led. Tasks are managed. The CEO's job is to steer the ship and make sure that we had experts throughout the organization that could execute their specialty and back up another specialty during vacations, illnesses, or force majeure situations where more than one person completing the task was required.

There are three types of managers:

The Enhancer: This is the manager who is self-confident, respected, responsible accountable, possesses personal power, and will get others to achieve results and accomplish organizational goals. The Enhancer is an authentic person that will take action and make focused decisions. Those that work with the Enhancer achieve results because they feel valued, worthwhile, and important. The Enhancer manages to turn crises into opportunities. They deliver value and play to win with measurable results.

The Neutralizer: This is a person capable of getting the work done. The Neutralizer has both respect from some and contempt from others. This person has limited self-confidence and delivers what the organization requires. Although they can laugh, cry, and display emotions, they typically don't. They lack personal power behind authority. You can anticipate what the Neutralizer will say and hope that you will not have to listen to them. Those that work for the Neutralizer toe the line. The Neutralizer delivers the status quo and maintains a neutral stance.

In some cases, this person creates a negative work environment. Their performance is adequate to mediocre. They may have absenteeism and turnover, but generally, the Neutralizer plays not to lose.

The Diminisher: This is a manager who lacks self-confidence and respect. The Diminisher is somewhat irresponsible. They use blame instead of accountability. They are powerless, rely on the authority of the position through threats and pressure people through intimidation to reach organizational goals. They don't laugh, cry, or get angry, and they have a difficult time showing empathy. The Diminisher will laugh at a superior's joke even if it is not funny. They are a threat to work with because their personal gains are achieved by manipulating others, and their excessive competitiveness creates distrust. They will stay on guard and collaborate with people of their same rank to keep up and protect themselves. The Diminisher is generally a burden on the organization because they drain more than they are paid. They are usually ineffective, show excess absenteeism, tardiness, and job turnover.

Goal-Setting Components

1. Listing your dreams. Where do you want to go with your job and your life?
2. Conducting Personal Self-Evaluations.
3. Developing Goal Categories.
4. Creating Goal Categories.
5. Creating Goal Statements.
6. Developing Specific Action Steps.
7. Prioritizing Your Goals and Action Steps.

Four Types of Goals:

1. Tangible goals can be firmly grasped.
2. Intangible goals relate to attitude, behaviors, personality traits, and skills that you want or need to develop.
3. Long-term goals should suit a specific longer span of time for your needs.
4. Short-term goals measure something you want to accomplish soon. These goals are barometers of confidence to achieve your long-term goals.

Criteria for Effective Goal Setting: WHYSMART

Written goals that clarify your thoughts and purpose

Harmonious with other goals, purpose, and vision

Your personal goals

Specific for clear direction

Measurable

Attainable so it will not lead to frustration

Realistic so that it is challenging but not beyond your capability to achieve

Time-bound goals set deadlines for expectations and motivation

Accountability: Goal Planning Sheet

Accountability is required to reach your goals. I have included an example planning sheet below. List your goals, rewards, consequences, target dates, today's date, and a positive affirmation. Include possible obstacles and solutions, necessary action steps with a date. Note if any of the action steps are delegated to another person. To achieve your goals, you must have a plan to be accountable to them.

https://achievemost.com/principles-of-cartel-disruption/

Organizing the Goal Process

A function of the executives in charge, as well as collaboration with the people that will carry out the actions to accomplish the goals, is to set department, division, or team goals. You can set company goals for quality, the output of work product, cost-effectiveness, absenteeism, safety, waste, new products and services, sales, marketing, and production management. The people in charge of setting the goals must have a belief that they are attainable.

People Management

Managing a group of people takes planning. Performance and attitude can make or break your organization. Here is a general way to approach it, but it may vary based upon your goals:

1. Communication: Upward, Downward, Lateral
2. Morale
3. Developing Subordinates
4. Career Path Planning
5. Delegation of Authority
6. Performance Appraisals
7. Discipline and Praise

Goals must be set in writing and tracked as you progress to lead your organization. You can use a time-use matrix to evaluate your efficiency in each of these areas of people management. Taking the right action with the right people for the right reasons is how you lead and develop platforms for the future.

Company Culture

A company's culture is a collection of self-sustaining patterns of behaving, feeling, thinking, and believing. The patterns determine the way things get accomplished in a company. An organization's culture is a potential source of value that enables, energizes, and enhances its employees and fosters high performance. When the culture is poor, it isn't easy to make successful strides towards your goals.

Common barriers to change and innovation include the following:

· Lack of data to make decisions
· Personal goals conflict with professional goals
· Management behavior discourages implementation
· Poor communication of vision, values, and mission
· Recognition and appraisals that are inconsistent with goals
· Unwillingness to develop new goals

Success comes when the organization's vision must be compelling and exciting to get through changing chaos. Data must support formal changes.

Action speaks louder than words, so make sure that your communication matches the resulting behavior. Learning new skills should be encouraged, and employees must be committed to the changes. Recognition and appraisals must be frequent and consistent with your values and mission. Finally, provide communication for each milestone you reach. As you create a team of leaders, heed the advice from the Innermetrix reports.

Be aware of the following roles:

- **The Navigator:** The Navigator clearly and quickly works through the complexity of issues. The individual is not rigidly entrenched in current policies and procedures.

- **The Enterprise Guardian:** This role ensures shareholder value through courageous decision-making that supports the enterprise and takes responsibility for unpopular decisions.

- **The Entrepreneur:** This role researches, identifies, and maximizes opportunities for new products, services, and new potential markets. The individual takes calculated risks to capitalize on emerging trends. The Entrepreneur looks beyond to grow and turns threats into opportunities.

- **The Mobilizer:** This role proactively aligns stakeholders, capabilities, and resources to get things done. The Mobilizer has a contingency plan and empowers others to achieve the strategy.

- **The Talent Advocate:** This role attracts, develops, and retains talent with the right skills and knowledge. The person creates developmental opportunities and minimizes barriers to achievement. The Talent Advocate builds a culture to facilitate employee development and retention.

- **The Captivator:** This role builds passion and commitment towards a common goal and conveys a simple yet vivid picture of the organization's vision and goals. The person generates energy and enthusiasm.

- **The Global Thinker:** This role integrates information from all sources to develop a diverse perspective that can be used and optimized by the organization's performance. The person understands different perspectives and approaches.

- **The Change Driver:** This role creates an environment that embraces change. The person recognizes the need to change before it is critical and embraces it.

- **The Right Action:** This role serves as a motivator and a leader. The focus is to understand how people will react to items that are required for success. This role assists people to reframe and transform their actions so that they can maximize their effectiveness. The person in this role must listen, observe, discern, model, and deliver! The person needs to be engaged, connected, clarify confusion, and gain commitment. The focus is to attain the right action by hiring and training the right people to do the right thing, the right way, at the right time, for the right reason. Yes, at times, it is easier said than done, but the focus should be on measurable incremental improvement and not perfection.

Visionary Leadership

Transformative visionary leadership is about purpose, direction, and inspiration. Leadership is about the relationship between people, leaders, and followers, which creates a firm foundation supported by values and trust. The key is to see where you envision yourself in five years. Then, you have to communicate your vision.

VISION + VALUES + CULTURE + COMMUNICATION = COMMITMENT

Leadership Communication Involves:

Mentor: Be a trusted advisor and tutor.

Believable: Be yourself and be authentic. If you can be read, you can be trusted.

Connect: Effectively communicating with exchanging ideas between two people.

Be Attentive: What people talk about is important to them.

Listen with an Open Mind: Approach a topic from the other person's point of view.

Keep an Eye Out for Feelings: Voice express feelings through pitch, intonation, hesitation, and speed of delivery. Pay attention!

Meaningful Feedback: This means active listening by showing genuine concern that reflects caring, empathy, and understanding. Find opportunities to complement, recognize, encourage, and praise. Move around the careless attitudes and nonverbal situations.

CHAPTER SIX

PRINCIPLE VI: Design and Improve Efficient and Effective Core Processes.

Lean Process Excellence: Cycle Chain and Variation Improvement

In organizations, there tends to be a lot of waste and inefficiencies that occur. From the beginning, chart out your processes to ensure that there is not waste. When you plan out all of your operations at the beginning, you are more likely to eliminate waste. Also, as you scale your business, these key components will aid your efforts to generate capital.

The cost of poor quality is extreme and can be found visibly and hidden:

HIDDEN AND UNHIDDEN WASTE | Chart 6.1

Visible:	Hidden Costs:
Excess overtime	Waste
Customer complaints	Grievances
Rework	Litigation
Billing errors	High turnover
Cost of quality assurance department	Low productivity
Consultants	Staff frustration
	Long cycle times
	Excessive accounts receivable
	Machine downtime
	Disability compensation
	Excessive inventories
	Missed schedules
	Incorrect order entry
	Lost customers
	Lack of teamwork between departments

To analyze your business so that you can attack issues of concern, I recommend holding an executive conference. It's an effective way to champion a system of continuous improvement and a focus on reducing and eliminating waste. The goal is to Define, Measure, Analyze, Improve, and Control (DMAIC) in a way that is Reasonable, Understandable, Measurable, Believable, and has Actionable outcomes (RUMBA).

Root Cause Analysis

Root Cause Analysis focuses on the elimination of variation without changing the process. It is a strategy of getting rid of the root causes of variation that are creating business problems. As an example, you may have a new customer service employee that gives uniformed information. You have customer service, but a better-implemented training procedure could help solve the issue. The focus should be on the universal root causes of variation of people, such as customers or coworkers. Other areas to consider are machines, test equipment, production equipment, databases, materials, and supplies. Review your protocols and procedures. Measurements such as bias and inaccuracy with data, as well as the working conditions and workplace organization, should be reviewed.

Cycle Time Reduction

Cycle Time Reduction (CTR) focuses on eliminating nonvalue-added steps, time, and improving workflow by changing the process. CTR focuses on the redesign of the workflow by refocusing functions, processes, and how things work from start to finish. Replace or change your processes to fix the problems. For example, to improve the flow and cost of egg processing, we had a machine that could dramatically increase the number of dozens and cases per staff hour. It reduced waste by having the machine check for cracked eggs instead of having humans do it inefficiently. These CTR changes occurred with the collaboration of engineers and people on the floor working to improve flow and cut down on waste. It has saved processors and farmers millions of dollars.

Team Charter

A team charter is a document that is developed as a group to clarify team direction while establishing boundaries. When forming a team, ground rules should be set for attendance, promptness, a set meeting time, participation, assignments to be carried out between meetings, acceptable interruptions, rotation of duties, and norms of behavior. The team charter effectively allows a team to clarify goals, educate and build the team, investigate the process, analyze the data and seek a solution, take appropriate action steps, and put forth in a report to management follow-up recommendations. In this exercise, the leader must clarify points, act as a gatekeeper, listen, focus the discussions, minimize digression, seek consensus, and continuously evaluate meetings and progress.

A team charter should define, measure, analyze, control, and improve a problem.

Common Elements of a Team Charter:

1. Process description
2. Corporate strategic objective
3. Goals
4. Team members
5. Process boundary beginning
6. Process boundary end
7. Criteria
8. Known failure mode
9. Measurement effectiveness
10. Measurement efficiency
11. Process input and suppliers
12. Process output
13. Internal customers
14. External customers
15. Process manager
16. Monuments commandments
17. Potential benefit
18. Management senior champion
19. Chartering review council

Variation Issues

Variation can be mapped out by using an Ishikawa Fishbone Diagram. It allows the team to brainstorm the root causes of a problem or issue within the business. The verbal data analysis tool displays possible causes of a specific problem, such as materials, people, methods, equipment, and environment. This tool allows a team to identify potential causes of a problem or issues like why customers are lost. If customers are lost, is it from poor customer service or a challenge like defective merchandise suddenly being produced? It's important not to jump to conclusions while developing a clear illustration of the possible cause of the problem.

BOX VARIATION ISSUE | Chart 6.2

Problem

Cycle Time

Another helpful strategy is to create an activity map and a product map with the current flow of products or services. It should also include the activities of the organization. Then create another version with no waste. Finally, create a practical flowchart to improve cycle time reduction. A focused team with leadership direction can solve the issues at times without bringing in an outside consultant. However, bringing in an external facilitator is an option that can help the organization overcome its current challenges.

ACTIVITY MAP AND PROCESS MAP PIZZA | Chart 6.3

Practical Example of How Activities, Ideal Process, Can Be Process, and Go To Process Gets Matriculated with a Team on a Wall

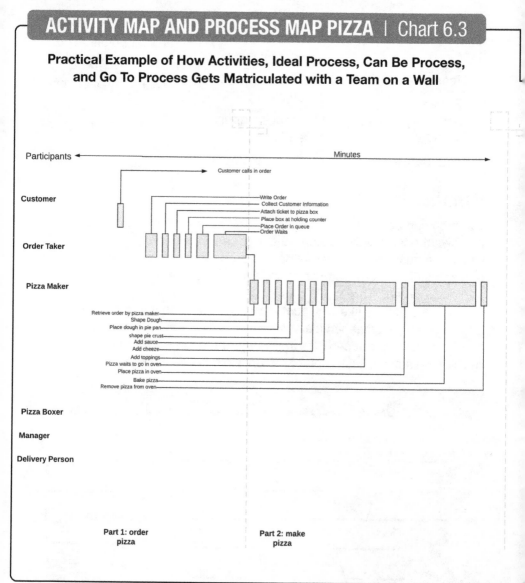

Participants ⟵——————————————————————— Minutes ——⟶

Customer

Customer calls in order

Order Taker

- Write Order
- Collect Customer Information
- Attach ticket to pizza box
- Place box at holding counter
- Place Order in queue
- Order Waits

Pizza Maker

- Retrieve order by pizza maker
- Shape Dough
- Place dough in pie pan
- shape pie crust
- Add sauce
- Add cheeze
- Add toppings
- Pizza waits to go in oven
- Place pizza in oven
- Bake pizza
- Remove pizza from oven

Pizza Boxer

Manager

Delivery Person

Part 1: order pizza

Part 2: make pizza

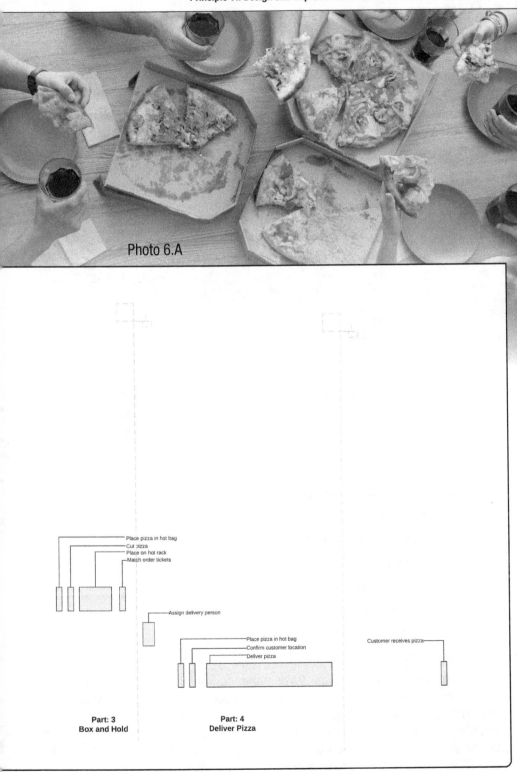

Photo 6.A

Place pizza in hot bag
Cut pizza
Place on hot rack
Match order tickets

Assign delivery person

Place pizza in hot bag
Confirm customer location
Deliver pizza

Customer receives pizza

Part: 3
Box and Hold

Part: 4
Deliver Pizza

Chart 6.3 (continued)

Process: Pizza order and delivery
Map begins: Customer calls in order
Map ends: Pizza delivered

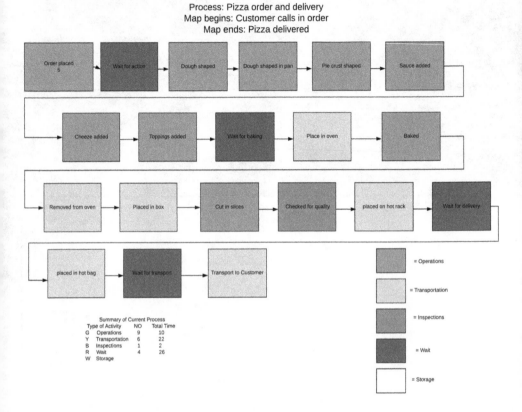

Summary of Current Process

Type of Activity		NO	Total Time
G	Operations	9	10
Y	Transportation	6	22
B	Inspections	1	2
R	Wait	4	26
W	Storage		

In summation, continuously engage in the following steps:

1. Identify opportunity
2. Form team and scope of project two
3. Analyze current as-is process
4. Determine entitlement
5. Identify ideal process
6. Create a *Can Be* process
7. Implement

Processes, teams, and structures must work in alignment. I have implemented this method in operations with our team and many others to save millions of dollars. It gets an organization aligned properly on process excellence, cutting out waste, and increasing quality using measurable data to analyze progress and success. In a recent project affiliated with a private equity firm, we were able to locate $10 to $15 million in savings from a waste walk, a flow diagram, and mapping out one process alone, which was the impetus of the change. The suggestion for change came from an employee who worked on the floor. She was happy to have her opinions heard. We were grateful for her insight!

Here is an actual simple example based upon lack of data collection that fell through the cracks:

1. Identify Opportunity: A fast-growing distributor of supplies does not have a method to handle returned merchandise. The current practice is to place returned merchandise in a designated area of the warehouse and then deal with it at a later time. The company's revenue was approaching $300 million. The people managing the task thought that returns were somewhere between 5 to 10 percent.

2. At an executive conference, a team of the operations manager and shipping manager, under the chief operating officer, who was the champion of the organization, assembled a team of two more people from the following areas: shipping, purchasing, customer service, and administration.

3. The current process for receiving the returned merchandise, storing, and then its disposal resulted in a $30 million loss.

4. Entitlements: The warehouse couldn't keep product for more than ten days due to storage space limitations.

5. Ideal Process: The ideal process would be that returned merchandise would result in a credit to the supplier plus a handling fee for the cost to do the work, plus 20 percent, plus a warehouse fee for merchandise housed during the time and storage. If a product has to be disposed of after ten days, the cost of the disposal would be credited to the supplier plus a 20 percent fee. There would be a fee for handling the merchandise as well. The cost of defective merchandise or mis-picks fell to the responsibility of the supplier.

6. The *Can Be* Process: The ideal process that cut out all of the waste and placed it all in the win column was not practical. The team believed it was best to research and work to renegotiate with the suppliers to create an industry-standard guaranteed sale provision or a return allowance of up to 10 percent. We agreed that this was not just an internal process of control. The management had the employees in the warehouse start tracking and measuring on a whiteboard the actual damage that was coming back. Then, they should translate the tracking by item in a spreadsheet for management and operations management review because data was needed. Management needed to be involved with suppliers to find a way to solve this issue.

7. As an interim solution, we immediately implemented putting returned shipments to a designated warehouse area. We tracked the data on the whiteboard and a spreadsheet. The department calls the supplier for a pickup and credit. This interim solution was to save $15 million based on early estimation. As additional data was collected, we adopted a guaranteed sale and return policy by the company and the supplier network based upon the integrity of knowing what was coming back.

In most situations, it is best to map these processes out on the wall by the team to identify the different tasks that need to be accomplished. Many challenges aren't as straightforward as this example. It can require a large team of operations workers and engineers to present their solutions to the senior management to cut waste and increase cash flow.

Lean Process Excellence in Action: Maine Culture Turnaround

To expand production to handle increased business due to a consumer boycott of a "bad boy" in the egg industry, we tackled a culture turnaround in individual facilities in Maine. Austin "Jack" DeCoster was an egg mogul. News reports alleged he was involved with facilities that sickened up to fifty-six thousand people in the Midwest. He served jail time for his role in such alleged sickness. The facilities we acquired were next door to DeCoster's remaining operation in Maine. We had purchased and leased the facilities about a decade before the issue occurred in the Midwest. At this time, several issues involving worker safety, wastewater treatment, food safety, and operational excellence were present.

To change the culture, we added a former engine room military and egg industry veteran named Tom Shea to the team. He was famous for working tirelessly, and he treated problems as opportunities. He led operational management and brought diversity and inclusion objectives to the operation.

We brought in an exceptional operational and technical business executive, Scott Burns, from Egg Fusion to tackle food safety and technological initiatives. The team was the best in the industry. It fought daily in the toughest of environments, considering the dysfunctional environment we were competing with next door. Eventually, we promoted Gay Smith to be the first woman to run a processing and production operation in Maine.

In our executive conference, we identified several areas to reduce waste and create variation improvement. The most significant area of improvement was how the eggs were handled. Inexperienced handlers routinely were not removing enough imperfections in eggs. This challenge caused quality issues with our customers, even after passing USDA inspection. As a quality-focused organization, we had higher expectations than USDA inspection.

Our initiative was to train our personnel better. The same was true with OSHA (Occupational Safety and Health Administration) safety issues. We developed a committee of employees that met regularly to discuss related issues. We created a strong relationship with the aid of expert OSHA consultant Deb Roy, OSHA Operational Director Sam Kondrup, and the area head, Bill Freeman.

In the early 2000s, the first OSHA inspection that made newspaper headlines revealed we had received no fines. The inspection was important to us because our neighbor DeCoster had received millions of dollars in fines, which caused him to lose most of his business due to a consumer boycott.

The same was true on wastewater treatment and nitrate runoff. We had John Engel of Engel Environmental do inspections to determine the nitrate runoff. We spent numerous amounts of time to make sure that our wastewater treatment was in line with the Maine Department of Environmental Protection (DEP) and the US Environmental Protection Agency (EPA). We also focused on the water quality for the workers and ensured testing regularly. This process took place after DeCoster received a consent order for wastewater treatment or lack thereof.

We worked with Dr. Mike Opitz and State Veterinarian Don Hoenig and Assistant State Veterinarian Beth McEvoy, along with Deputy Agriculture Commissioner Ned Porter, to ensure we were in line with the food safety requirements for the Maine Salmonella enteritidis risk reduction program.

We depopulated the production facility so we could adequately fill the mouse holes. Mice were carriers of Salmonella enteritidis. After baiting, we put forth appropriate cleaning. We eradicated Salmonella enteritidis with a lot of work. Scott Burns was crucial in implementing a comprehensive Food Safety Plan, including Safe Quality Food (SQF) inspections.

Scott and Tom said that they couldn't do their jobs because of the proximity of all of the industry's facilities in Maine. In his aircraft carrier engine room crisis voice, Tom Shea added appropriate color to the situation. New Jersey native Scott Burns characterized the issue stemming from Decoster's facilities as the "decision-making of Mad Men," which was reported in September 2010 by New England Cable News. Early on, Scott and Tom attempted to work without the state to remedy the biosecurity problems. Scott and Tom confronted their management at a meeting. They were concerned that if not rectified, the biosecurity situation could result in jail time for the management team. According to Scott, one of Decoster senior managers lifted his leg to show an ankle bracelet he was wearing for an alleged unrelated past transgression. The man smiled and said, "The worst that they could do to me is add more time on my ankle bracelet."

We enlisted the state with the help of Bill Bell of the New England Brown Egg Council, as well as industry veterans Julia and John Lough at the nearby Dorothy Egg Farms. I was president of the council, and Bill was executive director. We applied political pressure. It was a complicated task to eradicate Salmonella from farms in Maine. We did it and passed a later FDA inspection in 2010. Although it took strong leadership to implement process improvement and excellence, regardless of the obstacles, with proper guidance and a great team, it can and will happen!

CHAPTER SEVEN

PRINCIPLE VII: Learn and Implement the Power of Sustainability and Environmental, Social Governance.

Sustainability

What does sustainability mean worldwide? In a conference led by Costco and university professors I attended, we answered that question. If you clinically define sustainability, there are two separate meanings. The first is financial sustainability, which refers to the ongoing nature of a viable and profitable business. This type of sustainability requires your business systems to be in alignment. The second definition of sustainability refers to environmental implications. Stakeholders may have expectations for environmental sustainability, commonly referred to as being "green."

The Dilemma of Sustainability

Organizations are under increasing pressure from customers, investors, employees, legislators, banks, and insurance companies to embrace social and environmental concerns. Wall Street demands quarterly results, a stringent return on investment, and a short payback period. Studies increasingly show that the business benefits of sustainable strategies can be quantified and are real. Executives can review the bottom-line merits and are not necessarily tree huggers. Saving the world and making a profit is a proposition. It matters because your pain point is your customer's way, which is a purpose, cause, and belief that sustainability matters environmentally and businesswise.

Part of this process is defining what sustainability means to your client or organization. As an example, as noted by Steve Caballero, principal at US Alliance, "Sustainability is nothing more than the successful result of implementing a resource alignment strategy which increases productivity and reduces consumer resources without compromising profitability, competitiveness, or quality of your deliverable." The Brundtland Commission states that sustainability means meeting the needs of the present generation without compromising the ability of future generations to meet their own needs.

The goal is to identify fundamental principles to achieve technological breakthroughs that would lead to manufacturing without any form of waste and no emissions. When possible, transform materials considered to be waste into new products. This process can lead to new jobs and increased value. It causes industries that seem unrelated to cluster together. Waste and pollution are indicators of inefficiency. Inefficiencies tend to generate unneeded costs and environmental problems. Focus on achieving zero waste, toxins, emissions, and discharge. Waste elimination is achieved at the source through product design, producer responsibility, and waste reduction strategies down the supply chain. Some concepts to eliminate waste include cleaner production, product dismantling, recycling, reuse, and composting.

There is a significant amount of money to be made and saved in the area of sustainability. It can give you a competitive advantage and improve your brand image. Sustainability can also spur innovation. Once limited to corporate public relations, sustainability increasingly is seen by the world's leading companies as an imperative, not only good for the planet but directly equated with business value.

Implementation Model

Level 1

The organization is not ready to move forward.

Level 2

Initiate: Most companies don't know where to start. Level 2 is where you assess your company's level of sustainability. As you conduct an assessment, link your sustainability efforts to the strategic plan and how it will impact your stakeholders. Determine your current status and what improvements you would like to make.

Level 3

Implement: Create an implementation plan and put it into practice. Develop your people. Along the way, improve your processes to achieve a sustainable focus.

Level 4

Operationalize: To operationalize, focus on the outcomes you wish to achieve. What measurement can you put into place concerning your customers, employees, stakeholders, and shareholder loyalty?

Level 5

Transformation: Your organization becomes a steward of the environment, and you fully integrate sustainability into your culture. The organization now has a long-term vision and processes in place to continue a culture of sustainability.

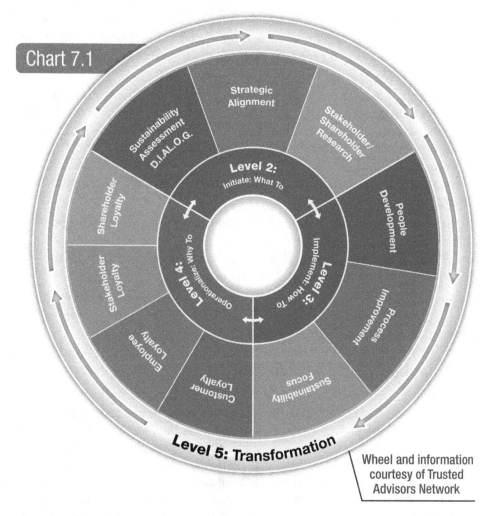

Chart 7.1

Strategic
Alignment

Sustainability
Assessment
D.I.AL.O.G.

Stakeholder/
Shareholder
Research

Shareholder
Loyalty

People
Development

Stakeholder
Loyalty

Level 2:
Initiate: What To

Level 4:
Operationalize: Why To

Level 3:
Implement: How To

Process
Improvement

Employee
Loyalty

Customer
Loyalty

Sustainability
Focus

Level 5: Transformation

Wheel and information
courtesy of Trusted
Advisors Network

Social Progress

Over the years, while growing Radlo Foods, we engaged in initiatives
that positively affected the social aspects of the business. Fifty-five
percent of our managers were women, including some of the first-
ever women production and processing managers in the US food and
agriculture industries, along with comptrollers, people resource managers,
administrators, executives, and board members. We employed exceptional
people of different races, nationalities, and political refugees before it was
fashionable to do so. We realized that there was a large talent pool that was
being underutilized. Diversity aligns itself with great success.

In another initiative, we created and accelerated Cage Free and later
Free Range eggs, along with humane dairy, chicken, and turkey. It made
sense to treat animals humanely and gain third-party certification for

Certified Humane and American Humane. It helped us deliver trust to our customers through verification. We also partnered in the development of nutritionally enhanced eggs, which included the great Egg-Land's Best and Born Free brands.

The economic impact, through billions of dollars in sales, brought a tidal wave of support in America through creating tens of thousands of jobs and sustaining hundreds of thousands of jobs. Employment was created through the supply chain from the new Cage Free, Free Range, and Organic Free Range barns, as well as reconstructed caged facilities, processors, feed supply and operations, truck drivers, sales, marketing, and customer service people.

The growth of exports included new market sales through relationships such as with the former Communist dictator Fidel Castro in Cuba. It brought great opportunities, profits, and anti-poverty efforts, along with other meaningful causes that work to repair the world.

Sustainability works for the greater good of any organization. It aligns environmental stewardship with waste reduction. Most importantly, it creates progress toward environmental and social improvement.

Lessons Learned: Right Action

The right alignment with the right action leads to success. You can have the right people focused on the right items, such as trends and messages in marketing, strategic business and planning, product development, marketing and pricing, promotion and sales, production, processing, and distribution. You do the right thing, the right way, and at the right time for the right reason. You attack the market with a vengeance ahead of the curve before the big boys catch up. You execute flawlessly in all phases of the game like in football, for example, offense, defense, and special teams (people, processes, strategy, and sustainability) with a competitive advantage to win. At the end of the day, you can unselfishly share the fruits of your labors with the ones that need it the most.

CHAPTER EIGHT

PRINCIPLE VIII: Use Operational Metrics to Guide Your Test Marketing and Early Stage Milestones.

Operational Metrics

Now we are moving from planning at the thirty-thousand-foot view to managing the ground game while operating. It's kind of like the difference between a game plan and game-time adjustments in sports. Every company has different policies and procedures. I am going to share with you one ground game lesson that aligns with sales, but it's important to have ground game lessons for every area of the business.

Here's what I learned from my experience in Fortune 100 Consumer Corporate land, Consumer Product Food Ag land, Biotech land, and, most recently Tec land. You are going to the test market shortly, but let's assume you will need salespeople. The best way to compensate salespeople is with a base salary plus a bonus structure based upon objective criteria. For me, it is aligning interests at all levels. For sales, it's incentivizing total revenue, unit revenue, incremental new distribution, and bottom-line profit. With these measures, the sales process is balanced between top-line growth, new business, and profits so that the salespeople don't have such a strong drive to reduce prices or increase promotions to a ridiculous level, as many companies pay according to top-line only.

Salespeople should manage their profit and loss for their area. They should chart out their sales plans for the following:

- What each customer is going to sell for the quarter
- Promotions
- Considerations for the cost to produce, brokerage, shrinkage

They also need to complete the wholesaler cost, their margin, and what it would cost the retailer. Then, an analysis is necessary to show costs to the retailer, sales, margins, fees, and price to the consumer on the shelf.

When salespeople's bonuses are based upon specific items such as bottom-line and new account acquisitions as well as top-line revenue, the company tends to make more money. This aligns the company and its growth.

Sales is challenging. When things go awry, it is usually in between the following stages. The first is motives, as stated above, and the second is execution, as indicated below in the sales flow process. It takes training, coaching, and motivation to develop great salespeople. We are all salespeople selling internally or externally in all that we do.

Test Markets

When going to market, you need to have what I call an operational metrics sheet (OMS) or multiple sheets for that fact. You require the cost to produce the product, the cost to supply the product to a distributor, and a percentage of shrinkage. You are responsible for the entire chain of the product getting to the customer. You need a spreadsheet for the distributor with their margins, costs, and price to their customers. Below is a sample sheet for Love It Ice Cream.

The goal here is to get you to start thinking beyond the planning stages. All of a sudden, you are thrust in the test market, where you need to start working on actual testing of revenue-based initiatives. Having a quantitative way to project and monitor results is essential. These test markets are also beneficial to show revenue and success that will help you raise additional capital by demonstrating a successful footprint. *(See Exhibit 8.1)*

Here are some other questions to consider:

- What is your base cost?
- What will be your cost when you have scale of production?
- Can you afford to price at scale of production and eat the difference or will you need to price your cost to begin or a hybrid of the two?
- What is your shrink projection?
- What is your cost to distribute?
- What is your cost to distribute directly to the customer warehouse?
- Is there any direct store delivery cost?
- Can you find a way to eat the cost of expensive distribution until you have volume?
- Do you have brokerage costs? What are they?
- What types of sales will you do? Can you sample products?
- What is the cost to do that?
- What is your plan to try out different approaches and discover how each works to drive trial and repeat purchase?
- What does your spreadsheet say? What does your customer say?

Sheet to Retailer

ICE CREAM

Product UPC	Size Pack	Case Pack	Promo Type	Cost to Winn Dixie	Deal per Unit	Net Unit	Est. Cases	Ad $ Per Unit	Less Ad $	Less Returns 2.5%	Less Broker 3.0%	$0.00	Less DSD $0.00	Shipping	Dead Net	Internal Cost to Produce	Profit	GP%
Blue Mountain 7 69123 30050 2	Quart	15	EDP	$1.690	$0	$1.690	300	$0	$1.690	$1.648	$1.598	$1.598	$1.598	$0.260	$1.338	$1.100	$0.238	14.10%
			SCAN	$1.690	$0.20	$1.490	500	$0.000	$1.490	$1.453	$1.409	$1.409	$1.409	$0.260	$1.149	$1.100	$0.049	3.30%
			AD	$1.690	$0.20	$1.490	500	$0.333	$1.157	$1.128	$1.094	$1.094	$1.094	$0.260	$0.834	$1.100	$0.266	-17.86%
Island Coconut 7 69123 51065 9	Quart	15	EDP	$1.750	$0	$1.750	300	$0	$1.750	$1.706	$1.655	$1.655	$1.655	$0.260	$1.395	$1.160	$0.235	13.43%
			SCAN	$1.750	$0.20	$1.550	500	$0.000	$1.550	$1.511	$1.466	$1.466	$1.466	$0.260	$1.206	$1.160	$0.046	2.96%
			AD	$1.750	$0.20	$1.550	500	$0.333	$1.217	$1.186	$1.151	$1.151	$1.151	$0.260	$0.891	$1.160	$0.269	-17.38%
Gummy Bears 7 69123 50897 7	Quart	15	EDP	$1.950	$0	$1.950	300	$0	$1.950	$1.901	$1.844	$1.844	$1.844	$0.260	$1.584	$1.260	$0.324	16.63%
			SCAN	$1.950	$0.20	$1.750	500	$0.000	$1.750	$1.706	$1.655	$1.655	$1.655	$0.260	$1.395	$1.260	$0.135	7.72%
			AD	$1.950	$0.20	$1.750	500	$0.333	$1.417	$1.381	$1.340	$1.340	$1.340	$0.260	$1.080	$1.260	$0.180	-10.30%
Watermelon 7 69123 62594 0	Quart	15	EDP	$2.810	$0	$2.810	250	$0.000	$2.810	$2.740	$2.658	$2.658	$2.658	$0.260	$2.398	$2.050	$0.348	12.37%
			SCAN	$2.810	$0.20	$2.610	400	$0.000	$2.610	$2.545	$2.468	$2.468	$2.468	$0.260	$2.208	$2.050	$0.158	6.07%

ICE CREAM CHIPS

Product UPC	Unit Size	Case Pack	Promo Type	Cost to Winn Dixie	Deal per Unit	Net Unit	Est. Cases	Ad $ Per Unit	Less Ad $	Less Returns 1.0%	Less Broker 3.0%	Less Etching $0.00	Less DSD $0.00	Shipping	Dead Net	Internal Cost to Produce	Profit	Love it GP%
Chocolat Chip 7 69123 60086 2	Bags	8	EDP	$2.190	$0	$2.190	250	$0	$2.190	$2.168	$2.103	$2.103	$2.103	$0.310	$1.793	$1.590	$0.203	9.27%
			SCAN	$2.190	$0.20	$1.990	300	$0.000	$1.990	$1.970	$1.911	$1.911	$1.911	$0.310	$1.601	$1.590	$0.011	0.55%
			AD	$2.190	$0.20	$1.990	400	$0.417	$1.573	$1.534	$1.488	$1.488	$1.488	$0.310	$1.178	$1.590	$0.412	-20.70%

Promo Fees	
SCAN:	$0
AD:	$2,500
SLOT:	$25,000

Margins are from 30% to 40% depending on the potential volume

LOVE IT! ICE CREAM SALES OPS SHEET | Chart 8.2

Retailer Sheet

ICE CREAM

Product UPC	Size Pack	Case Pack	Promo Type	Retail	Case Cost	Total Deal	Net Case	Net Unit	GP%	Est. Cases	Ad Fee	Ad $ Per Unit	Dead Net Per Unit
Blue Mountain 7 69123 30050 2	Quart	15	EDP	$2.69	$25.35	$0	$25.35	**$1.690**	37.2%	500	$0	$0	$1.690
			SCAN	$2.29	$25.35	$3.00	$22.35	**$1.490**	34.9%	800	$0	$0.000	$1.490
			AD	$1.99	$25.35	$3.00	$22.35	**$1.490**	25.1%	1,000	$2,500	$0.167	$1.323
Island Coconut 7 69123 51065 9	Quart	15	EDP	$2.79	$26.25	$0	$26.25	**$1.750**	37.3%	500	$0	$0	$1.750
			SCAN	$2.49	$26.25	$3.00	$23.25	**$1.550**	37.8%	800	$0	$0.000	$1.550
			AD	$2.29	$26.25	$3.00	$23.25	**$1.550**	32.3%	1,000	$2,500	$0.167	$1.383
Gummy Bears 7 69123 50897 7	Quart	15	EDP	$3.19	$29.25	$0	$29.25	**$1.950**	38.9%	500	$0	$0	$1.950
			SCAN	$2.79	$29.25	$3.00	$26.25	**$1.750**	37.3%	800	$0	$0.000	$1.750
			AD	$2.59	$29.25	$3.00	$26.25	**$1.750**	32.4%	1,000	$2,500	$0.167	$1.583
Watermelon 7 69123 62594 0	Quart	15	EDP	$4.29	$42.15	$0	$42.15	**$2.810**	34.5%	400	$0	$0	$2.810
			SCAN	$3.89	$42.15	$3.00	$39.15	**$2.610**	32.9%	700	$0	$0.000	$2.610

ICE CREAM CHIPS

Product UPC	Unit Size	Case Pack	Promo Type	Retail	Case Cost	Total Deal	Net Case	Net Unit	GP%	Est. Cases	Ad Fee	Ad $ Per Unit	Dead Net Per Unit
Chocolate Chip	Bags	8	EDP	$3.49	$17.52	$0	$17.52	$2.190	37.2%	400	$0	$0	$2.190
			SCAN	$2.99	$17.52	$1.60	$17.52	$1.990	33.4%	600	$0	$0.000	$1.990
			AD	$2.50	$17.52	$1.60	$17.52	$1.990	20.4%	800	$2,500	$0.208	$1.782

Promo Fees	
SCAN:	$0
AD:	$2,500
SLOT:	$25,000

Pricing Subject to Quarterly Review

· How many units of product do you intend to sell, at what price, and therefore what is your revenue that you project based upon everyday sales? How about when promotions begin? Volume up 30 percent, 50 percent after promotions? Building repeat customers? Is there a bump?

· How much can you spend to gain trial and judge repeat?

- How do you intend to measure the promotions?

- What does your online and conventional advertising plan look like? Are you going to defer that until you have a better read in basic test? Can you?

- What are the minimum sales needed to stay in the game with your wholesale, retailer, or an online customer platform?

The base of doing a test market is running different scenarios and see what works. With a retail food product, you can start with a few stores, but you want to get to a market test of about five hundred stores to gauge results to get a fair representation. It all depends on what is in your budget. Can you demonstrate a sustainable business model with enough unit margin so it could be a footprint that can be accelerated?

We are not even into sales, general, and administrative expenses as well as property, plant, and equipment expenses. Remember, this is just a base operational exercise to see if contribution can be successfully sustained in a test.

As your business grows and develops into a more mature framework, the qualitative side is getting your people to align with the company. You have to pay them incentive compensation and rewards of all sorts, which include praise, coaching, and encouragement! Your goal is to create alignment with the results you are seeking.

The same is true for every part of your business. If you must make 99 percent fulfillment of the product ordered, 6 sigma (3.4 defects per million opportunities), or 0 defects, then you must set up systems so that everyone is compensated and rewarded for meeting such goals. This is not just money. It includes awards, recognition, and organized systematic checks. Many businesspeople don't look at these components until after they have the funding and move to set up their operation. Some operations don't look at the components until they lose business, which is worse than the previous scenario.

This chapter is short on words but long on principle. If you can't find a way in the test phase to make the value proposition work, it's time to redo the test, assess for better timing, or move on and be straight with all parties involved. There is no need to spend good money after bad test market results. If you can get great results from the test, then you are proving that you are in a high-growth segment of a large market and the timing is right.

Figure 8.3 shows an example for a year one projected total for profit and loss for Love It Ice Cream as it is rolled into the company's financials. You will also see how the overall company turns a profit in 2020 and chugs along to project the next two years. It is imperative to do detailed cash flow analysis as well, so you are not P&L positive and run out of cash. You don't

ANNUAL SHEET	PROJECTIONS SALES	2020 % SLS	AVERAGE PER UNIT	Ave Time Cash Turn	Actual 2018	Actual 2019	Projected 2020	Projected 2021	Projected 2022
UNITS SOLD 4,000,000									
GROSS SALES	$11,100,000	100%	$2.78	30	0	5550000	$11,100,000	$15,762,000	$24,431,100
Total Promo Spend	$456,000	4%			100000	400000	$456,000	$647,520	$1,003,656
Total Trade	$456,000	4%			100000	450000	$456,000	$647,520	$1,003,656
Net Sales	$10,188,000	92%	$2.55	30	$(200,000)	$4,700,000	$10,188,000	$14,466,960	$22,423,788
Other Trade									
Royalty if Any									
Cost of Goods	$4,500,000	41%		10	$50,000	$2,250,000	$4,500,000	5989560	9283818
Other Including Doubtful Accounts					$62,000				
Gross COG	$4,500,000	41%			$112,000	$2,250,000	$4,500,000	5989560	9283818
Exchange Rate if any									
Total COG	$4,500,000	41%	$1.13	10	$112,000	$2,250,000	$4,500,000	5989560	9283818
Transport-Wholesale	346,844	3%	$0.09	15	0	260,133	346,844	472,860	732,933
Brokers Fees	132,418	1%	$0.03	30	0	66,209	132,418	157,620	244,311
Damage Returns	176,656	2%	$0.04	7	0	88,328	176,656	315,240	488,622
Distribtor Costs	406,650	4%	$0.10	15	20000	203,325	406,650	444,000	630,480
DIRECT COSTS:	$1,062,568	10%	$0.27		$20,000	$617,995	$1,062,568	$1,389,720	$2,096,346
DIRECT TRADE CONTRIBUTION	$4,625,432	42%	$1.16		$(332,000)	$1,832,005	$4,625,432	$7,087,680	$11,043,624
All Consumer Support	$1,500,000	14%	$0.38	30		$1,500,000	$1,500,000	$1,800,000	$2,000,000
Listing or Slotting Fees	$252,400	2%	$0.06	30		$300,000	$252,400	$500,000	$750,000
CONSUMER AND SLOTTING	$1,752,400	16%	$0.44	30	$ -	$1,800,000	$1,752,400	$2,300,000	$2,750,000
CONTRIBUTION MARGIN	$2,873,032	26%	$0.72		$(332,000)	$32,005	$2,873,032	$4,787,680	$8,293,624
OTHER COSTS:									
Sales, General, and Admin(SGA)	1100000	10%	$0.28	7	$110,000	$110,000	750,000	850,000	850,000
Property, Plant, and Equipment	200000	2%	$0.05	30	$50,000	$50,000	200,000	200,000	200,000
Depreciation, Amoritzation, Interest	500000	5%	$0.13	30	$60,000	$60,000	195,000	195,000	195,000
TOTAL OTHER:	1800000	16%	$0.45		$220,000	$220,000	$1,145,000	$1,245,000	$1,245,000
NET NET*	$1,073,032	10%	$0.27		$(552,000)	$(187,995)	$1,728,032	$3,542,680	$7,048,624

want to contact your financial lenders and equity holders for a cash call, especially during the holidays, because of poor planning even with positive results. You likely won't get a callback. The profit and loss are on the left, and the key per unit indicators are on the right. You will learn to focus on these costs and find a bottom line as you make projections. Then you will compare your actual results to your forecasts.

Milestones

I want to share a quick word on milestones. When you are building your IP, every step of the way builds value and confidence. For example, when the patent office accepts a pending patent, you have a scientifically proven principle. This opportunity brings forth proof of stability. Another example of building value is when a scientific study comes back with positive results. These examples are great milestone objectives that build value and excitement and add value to the business.

https://achievemost.com/principles-of-cartel-disruption/

CHAPTER NINE

PRINCIPLE IX: Understand Your Exit Opportunities and Develop a Strategy to Make It Happen.

The best exit strategy is one that meets the business goals and financial needs for you and your partners. There are many options. For example, if you have a legacy goal, you might transfer your business to your children and grandchildren. There is a distinction between ownership and management. Still, management should have significant upside opportunities and incentives that align with ownership, such as Restricted Stock Awards (RSA), Employee Stock Ownership Plans (ESOP), and Profit Sharing. For this option, I have seen fifty-to-one-hundred-year plans. For early-stage and venture capital, you are generally looking at a five-to-seven-year target. Private equity is a sprint. In this situation, the time frame is three years, with a maximum of seven years in some cases.

It's important to consider an exit strategy early in your process instead of waiting until there is a problem or there is a situation like challenges of liquidity, profitability, efficiency, or lack of succession planning and different partner expectations that would call for you to exit. Creating a transition plan will create less stress when you and your partners decide it's time to move on to new ventures and can certainly and should be part of strategic planning but sometimes gets left out.

Exit Strategies

Merger and Acquisition (M&A): The basic definition of M&A is to merge with a similar company or to be bought out by another company. The goal here is synergistic win-win when bordering companies have complementary skills and can save resources by combining. For larger organizations, it's a more efficient way to grow their revenue than to create new products. They still may have an organic pipeline, but they also have an inorganic target list of acquisitions. There are always suitors out there.

Initial Public Offering (IPO): Depending on the trend, it is in or it is out. The IPO rate has shown declines. Shareholders are demanding, and liability concerns might be great. Also, if you exit, there is generally a blackout period before you can liquidate your shares, and you will no longer be in control. If you can't manage it, you can't control it, and you shouldn't have to worry about it.

Sell to an Individual: When you sell to an individual, be ready to pay off your investors. The ideal buyer may or may not be someone who has the skills and interest on the operational side of the business. Scaling can be a challenge. You can alternatively sell a noncontrolling stake to a strategic or financial partner to gain the liquidity that you require while staying in control.

Make It Your Cash Cow: Use estate planning to turn it over to future generations. If you are in a stable, secure marketplace with a business that has a steady revenue stream, you can pay off investors and find someone you trust to run it for you, which may or may not be related family members. With the remaining cash, you can develop new ventures in organic or inorganic growth. You retain ownership and enjoy the annuity. A cash cow seems to need constant feeding to stay healthy, and it's essential to have trusted attorneys work to ensure the most favorable legal and tax situation for your family. Meredeth Beers of Holland & Knight is probably the best in the business on estate planning.

Liquidation and Close: Shut the business down. Take the cash. Liquidate and pay off your people. Then go fishing or eat a vegan burger.

Valuation 101

Value is an estimation of something's worth. The market basis of supply and demand, like ice cream or peanuts, is the same for a business. Supply and demand and a great marketing package can determine the worth. An excellent way to start is to consider what you would pay for it. Then, get an expert fairness opinion to back up the value based on industry norms.

There are different ways of valuing businesses. Explore your local VC, I-banker, corporate finance professor, or financial expert. You can sell assets or IP value based on where it is in the pipeline in terms of milestones and prospects for later value on development. You can also sell the stock of the company, which includes the assets and liabilities.

Generally, the more stable low growth of the company, the lower of the multiple on the sale. The higher the growth, the higher the multiple. That's why I started this book with the suggestion that you have a fast-growing segment of a large market. What I mean by multiple is the X times sales, X times, EBITDA, X times contribution margin. X times EBITDA plus specified assets such as cash and assets. There is a lot more that goes into this, but this will get you started thinking.

The basic rule of thumb is that a cash flow basic business with slow growth below 10 percent YOY means annual growth would trade around three to five times yearly EBITDA. However, higher growth companies that have a killer value proposition with IP that grow a combined EBITDA and YOY growth over 40 percent will garner high multiples above 10X times EBITDA. Another example of alternative value creation pre-revenue is a blockbuster technology such as curing a life-threatening disease like Parkinson's or cancer as it moves towards FDA approval and key milestones achieved as discussed earlier without any revenue at all.

Another high multiple larger private equity business, for example, is to have "a roll-up strategy in the can" with several acquisition targets and actual acquisitions that will significantly increase in value in two ways. The first is straight additional revenue and profits through acquiring the businesses. The second way is through a mechanism called arbitrage. You might be able to buy a company at 3–5X earnings, but if your overall growth rate is high, you might be able to sell the entire company later for 10X plus. In this situation, you are doubling or tripling the previous acquisition through arbitrage. In most cases, investment bankers that act as intermediaries will significantly aid in the process.

Remember, your investors are expecting a return on their money, which includes your friends and family. The investors typically get their return when they cash out or the company is sold. Investors look for several traps when they consider investing in companies. As a reminder, I have the Seven Deadly Sins of Private Equity Investors posted on my wall.

For those of you that love crowdfunding, here is my take on it. It is a newly developing service, and I hope it does well. It has proven to be a great way of giving back and rallying for a cause such as a natural disaster or other charitable endeavors.

In some circumstances, companies like Kickstarter have been successful in raising funds as an alternate vehicle for ventures. It's not for everyone, so please do a competitive analysis on the industry, review the company's offerings, and their record for success. Crowdfunding provides an immediate means of valuation because it is an online instrument, and people are willing to pay X amount for Y value.

The Seven Deadly Sins of Private Equity Investors

Envy: Don't covet your neighbor's platform or assets. You may be under the dangerous impression that life gets easier when you have what others have. Just because your competitors look like they are doing well doesn't mean they are. Don't focus on playing their games. Focus on playing yours.

Lust: The desire to pursue a CEO who at first seems like a rock star and Jedi Knight can be the smoke and mirrors that attract your attention. Believing this one individual can fix all of your problems and increase your profits astronomically can be alluring. The reality can be sobering. Many professionals have pursued a go-getter executive with offers of uncapped bonuses, accelerated equity grants, and more. The challenge is that these people sometimes have baggage like a hoarder on a road trip.

Gluttony: Don't become the culprit of overzealous strategies. The more debt you take on, the more significant your gains, but can you guarantee the market will change the way you see fit? Too much debt will narrow your long-term options. Your debt can pull you down like an anchor.

Greed: Listen to your limited partners, and don't do too many things at the same time. Private equity is a marathon, not a sprint. Instead of falling prey to greed, substitute this sin for the virtue of patience.

Pride: It is rare for associates, principals, and partners alike to keep up appearances, because no one wants to appear foolish, which ironically is the most foolish thing you can do. It's better to ask the questions and deal with the jokes or teasing. When you don't ask the questions or address your concerns, you run the risk of mistakes that could have been avoided by speaking up. As cliché as it sounds, there are no stupid questions.

Sloth: The inability to make difficult decisions is not lethargy. When the market changes, the CEO must take new action. Teddy Roosevelt said that in any situation, the best thing you can do is the right thing, the next best thing is the wrong thing, and the worst thing you can do is nothing.

Wrath: There are many examples of markets hurling their fury against an investment. You can't avoid it at times. Hunker down and wait for the storm to pass.[8]

CHAPTER TEN

PRINCIPLE X: Select a Talented Board of Directors and Advisors to Help Accelerate Growth Based on the Needs of the Business.

The purpose of board members is to complement and protect you. Choose people with diverse backgrounds, age levels, and fields. Diversity will assist you in gaining unique perspectives as you move forward. Choose an odd number of total members, so when it comes time for a vote, you will receive clear feedback. Your board has significant influence over decisions, so choose wisely. Seek people who are strategic thinkers, creative problem solvers, and leaders. Have key people with finance experience to protect your organization. Board members should add value to the business in a meaningful way. It should not be seen as easy money for a few meetings. However, nonvoting advisors can also fill the gaps quite well.

As an entrepreneur or leader, it is vital to choose the best advisors and board members that add value to the organization. You should also select an outstanding team with complementary talents.

In my organizations, diversity and women were in the majority because they were exceptionally talented people. Sandy Porter, Stephanie Norton, Gay Smith, Nicky Dunagan, Charlene Mooney, and Christine Bushway are a few of the outstanding women with whom I've worked. I learned this early in my life. My mother was in the last graduating class of Radcliffe Management School before women were allowed into Harvard Business School. My dad hired the first African American senior processing manager in Gainesville, Georgia, in the late 1960s and 1970s, while many in the South were working on integration plans.

When my senior VP of operations, Tom Shea, and I hired a group of Somali Muslim refugees on September 11, 2001, in Leeds, Maine, at our plant, Tom feared a backlash after seeing the planes crash into the World Trade Center. We did not waiver and solidly stood behind them. I told Tom to spread the word that we had hired political refugees and that they were peaceful and hardworking people. We welcomed them with open arms. I told Tom that if anyone had issues, they could call or see him or me directly or inquire with the VP of administration and human resources, Stephanie

Norton, after they read their human resource manual on our policy of nondiscrimination. We didn't have any issues and made sure that the new employees had a safe and appropriate place to pray five times per day.

Depending on the size of the company, you will attract a variety of people. The needs of the business require an array of opinions. With smaller entrepreneurial ventures, big funders might request board seats. Private equity-acquired ventures generally appoint outside board members along with a few from the private equity company so it can have control of the business. With larger corporations, the likely selection is with accountants, bankers, and at times a specialist or CEO or former CEO. It can lead to blind spots and too much silo thinking. An unbiased skills analysis is required of boards. Base the review on the functions needed. As an entrepreneur, you can start with the objective of filling in holes with a board and advisors that complement each other and can help management with issues based upon their specialty. If you can't get directors to fill the gaps, then advisors will do.

Board and Advisory Board

To have a successful company, you need rock star board members and advisors. The board must cover all necessary functions in the advisory that include: Leadership, Finance, Communications/PR, Government, and Regulatory, Strategy Formation/Execution, Merger/Alliance/Acquisition, Governance, Technical Knowledge, Compensation, Risk Assessment, Industry Knowledge, and Board Compatibility. There should be a balance in alignment with the organization's needs to keep you moving in the right direction with the right action.

While I was president and CEO of Radlo Foods (Egg-Land's Best and Born Free Eggs, among many other eggs, foodstuffs, and biotech), I was able to pick up some outstanding talent to create an exceptional board. Any Fortune 500 company would desire this group of extraordinary people. My focus was to support blockbuster organic growth. I am going to walk you through my rock star board so you can see how they fit together and how the balance was achieved.

Martha Guidry: Martha was the most exceptional thought leader in consumer market research. She is a former P&G product manager and Harvard Business School graduate. She did an outstanding job of identifying the target market and drivers to meet customer trends and pain points. The success of our food business started with Martha at every turn, so we could leanly assess from target customer engagement and learn our best right action from consumer reactions. Martha is worth her weight in gold.

Tony DeLio: I met Tony DeLio in Cuba when he was president of the nutraceutical division at ADM. Tony is now the chief innovation officer at Ingredion (National Starch). Tony is a true rock star and was great with strategic assistance and product formulations throughout the business. He was integral in attaining our joint venture with Cargill later on where we were both co-patent holders to technology. His strategic guidance on significant issues was exceedingly valued. He joined us when he left Archer Daniels Midland to become the vice chancellor of the University of Chicago before he went to National Starch. Overall strategy and research and development (R&D) was his specialty, and now he runs mergers and acquisitions (M&A) and Innovation for the $6 billion company Ingredion.

Bob Goehrke: I met Bob when I was at NYU, and he was a senior executive at Clairol along with his Tufts Delta Upsilon (DU) best friend, Peter Dolan, who was the VP of marketing at Bristol-Myers Squibb before becoming president. They were both DU fraternity brothers that were kind enough to see this MBA student. After they saw me, I gave them a Tufts DU tie, which they appreciated. I kept up with Bob through the years. When I found out that he was in the middle of change and running a consulting company called Dream Team Marketers, I immediately engaged Bob to be on my board. He brought Mark Shuster with him.

Bob is now cooking as CEO of International Products Group with his wife Tish, based out in Salt Lake City, Utah, and his sales have doubled the past couple years by adding CBD cream to the mix of products worldwide. Their firm IPG Group (International Products Group), is now the best innovative firm in bath and beauty in the world.

Jorge Santos: Jorge Santos worked with Tony DeLio at Mars, Incorporated. He was outstanding in marketing planning and development. Jorge was also a Mars country head in Portugal. I am currently a board member, and my company is a shareholder in Jorge's cannabis- and Parkinson's-related bioscience technology company in Toronto, Canada. I have been blessed that I have been able to continue to work with Jorge post-Radlo Foods. He is a dynamic and successful entrepreneur now and not just a big hotshot corporate executive. I have been privileged to be able to mentor and coach him. Jorge was great at marketing and long-term strategic and financial planning with new technology, ventures, and products.

Mark Shuster: Mark Shuster was the former VP of marketing for both Converse and Old Mother Hubbard. He was a creative marketing executive with a strong focus on market implementation and an NYU Stern School of Business graduate. He worked with Joan Leroy, the senior director of marketing, daily and weekly, as needed in that regard as a strong engine of consistent ideas and growth. I was blessed to have Mark.

Dave Gorman: Dave Gorman oversaw the board's risk management, audit, and operations. He assisted greatly with cultural development. He was also fundamental in ensuring that we had the right operational and administrative platforms for growth. Dave was the former head of loss prevention and quality assurance at Walmart stores. He was a former Marine and Sam Walton's auditor. As noted earlier, Dave was the person who taught Sam Walton how to use a cell phone and was there during Walmart's tremendous rise to growth. I owe much to Dave Gorman and not just by him saving my Walmart business when it got into trouble, but also for keeping an eye out that everything and everyone was moving down the right path. He was a champion who pounded on eliminating waste and operating a lean operation that reduced cycle time, variation waste, and inefficiencies. He also watched for unnecessary insurance risks.

Many companies have five of Dave Gorman on the board. I learned early on that it took five people to take Dave Gorman's position at Walmart. I figured I could use him to multitask on my board as he did at Walmart on my board. He was an excellent counterbalance to the board of growth executives. At times, Dave drove my CFO, Paul Gisborne, crazy, but he worked quite well with the operations, finance, administration, and technical management teams. We needed Dave Gorman to execute organizational excellence. He did a great job and interfaced with accountants John Burke and Tony Russo.

John Hampton: Over the years, John Hampton and I have had a lot of fun on adventures in New York, the Bahamas, Florida, New England, and Cuba. John had a high-risk tolerance and unfortunately got caught up in the mortgage meltdown crisis, which drastically affected his real estate business in Florida around the same time that he beat cancer. John has been through the wringer and gets up smiling. He is always a southern gentleman. He's exceedingly bright and was a great addition to an outstanding board.

John was very instrumental in some of our mergers and acquisitions. He also assisted with mergers and acquisitions finance and inorganic integration. Real estate was his specialty, so he helped with our real estate transactions. I've always believed in the General Electric (GE) model for acquisitions. Also, it would be best if you had a generalist like myself paired up with a finance professional and a great attorney. At times GE uses more, but this is a good model. John has been great at filling the inorganic finance role.

Stephanie Norton: Stephanie Norton has had the role of my VP of administration and human resources. She continues to manage my administration and work on all people-related issues. She was also the secretary of the board, and she had a levelheaded, calming influence. I was told that people would rather talk to her than talk to me most of the time.

One of Stephanie's first assignments was to corral a twenty-six-member delegation of ours to go to Cuba during the early 2000s. We were an exhibitor at the Food Expo. There was also a reception in Old Havana, and she kept all parties in order. Fidel Castro was always a charmer. He gave Stephanie flowers after we finished having a private dinner with him at the Presidential Palace.

Paul Gisbourne: Paul Gisbourne was our CFO and comptroller. Paul was efficient, accurate with his statements, and always prepared for audits.

Gus Schumacher: Gus Schumacher and I grew up in Lexington, Massachusetts. He was a great friend of the family until his recent passing. He was undersecretary of Agriculture for Farm and Farm Services at the USDA during the Clinton administration. He was also a former Massachusetts State Agriculture secretary. Gus helped to boost our reputation and stature throughout the food and food safety industry. Reputation is critical to any successful enterprise, and Gus did an outstanding job bolstering our stature and reputation. He was always pointed and direct with his advice.

Christine Bushway: Chris Bushway has served in numerous leadership capacities in the egg industry and the Organic Trade Association. She also ran a consulting firm that was in partnership with the American Egg Board. Chris helped with the growth of our company in the earlier years. She was able to leanly get things done with the assistance of her partner, the late, great Ron Mills.

John Brzezenski: John Brzezenski, also known as "Ski," played football on one of Bill Tighe's teams. Coach Tighe, whom I also played for and coached with, is the longest-serving high school coach in history. He also fought heroically in the battle of Iwo Jima when my dad was fighting in Europe under Patton in WWII. John was an outstanding football player at Harvard. He later went on to Harvard Business School.

John is an expert in growth management consulting for tech companies. He was a great addition to our board. John and his wife, Lisa Pizzutti Brzezenski, are well respected in the Boston real estate arena, and his sister-in-law Linda Pizzutti Henry is managing director of the *Boston Globe* with her husband, John Henry, who also owns and runs the Boston Red Sox. Ski is one of the most tech-savvy, levelheaded people that I know. He will bend your ear about the importance and emergence of electric vehicles for sustainability and practicality.

Sheldon Hendler: Sheldon Hendler was a distinguished professor at the University of California. He worked with Tony DeLio at ADM. Sheldon assisted with patent development and the creation of healthier foods with higher-quality ingredients.

Dan Rogers: Danny was the former chairman of the USA Poultry & Egg Export Council. He drove my good friend Jim Sumner, president of the Council (and later World Poultry Federation president) crazy at times. His expertise was strategic, tactical management on ventures and alliances. He has an outstanding ability to handle details in strategic ventures. Dan still works with me to this day.

Unofficial Help:

Trusted advisors that aren't officially on your board are also needed. These people usually will always shoot you straight with particular issues within their domain. I turn to my attorney friends Kevin Cloherty, Rob Friedman, and Josh Brown. They are outstanding attorneys in their own right.

Kevin is now deputy general counsel of John Hancock-Manulife after a notable career with the Justice Department and US Attorney's office fighting public corruption and organized crime. He was the head of the New England Organized Crime Strike Force. Rob Friedman is a former district attorney in Brooklyn, New York. Today, he's a senior corporate lawyer at Sheppard Mullin in New York, and I highly recommend him. Josh is the best junkyard dog in the Branford/New Haven area. He handles debt issues, foreclosures, etc.

These guys razz me when I ask them for advice. Together, with a box or two of Cubans, a few beers, cape sunsets, golf courses, and football games, I learn a few things. We also tend to have more fun than do actual work.

I tie in from time to time with Mark Micciche, Rick Lerner, Kevin Baker, Bif Crowley, Dan Doherty, Brian Kavoogian, Mark Andon, and Brian McGrail. In the food industry, Doug Richardson, Greg Hinton, Marcus Rust, and Jim Sumner are a few that deserve mention. Doug is the chairman of Moore, Stevens, and Frost. His firm is the official auditor of most agriculture businesses in America. His team is well respected in the industry, and it was great working with them concerning food-ag support issues. He's a savvy accountant and businessman. Greg is the VP of sales and marketing for Rose Acre Farms. He is also the incoming president of the International Egg Commission. Marcus Rust is the chairman and CEO of Rose Acre Farms. Both of them are great friends and supporters of the entrepreneurial cause, as was "friendversary" Mike Culley, chairman of CMC Food in New Jersey. My partner at NYU Stern, Lisa Fraser, has been wonderful for bouncing ideas off of over the years as well.

Paul Sauder, owner of R.W. Sauder, from Lititz, Pennsylvania, bought into the dream before it was a dream. Paul's Lancaster County neighbor, Ron Kreider, owner of Kreider Farms, jumped down to Cuba with me. Jim Sumner has been president of Chicken World and president of the USA Poultry & Egg Export Council that initially pestered me to get down to Cuba and meet with Castro on a trade mission. I will give due credit to an outstanding entrepreneur, Jacques Klempf. He sold his EB partnership interest and egg production business at a very high value and invested in, and runs, the best food and entertainment venue in Jacksonville, Florida, Cowford Chophouse, with his wife, Tracy. I learned much from him. Special note to my fiancé, Anne Winkler, a rock an anchor to me and an accomplished ICU and CCU Social worker in her own right.

Skills Gap Review: Case Study

A skills gap review examines a board or advisory board's weaknesses and uncovers opportunities for improvement. The goal is to see what is missing to incrementally improve. I am going to walk you through a case study company so you can see the importance of this type of review.

The case study company had a nine-member board with one vacancy. The board was overloaded with compensation and audit members but lacked other vital support in financial and legal professionals. The president and CEO, CFO, and COO were all board members as well. I completed a skills analysis based on a few missing pieces.

They needed a specialist for IT/Cyber; however, they lacked a generalist accelerator. Members with general management skills were lacking as well as a proactive, nonorganic committee to deal with acquisitions, sales, mergers, and divestiture. I also found there was not a standard executive committee. There was no one to assist with executive direction, which was a challenge. Upon the excellent advice of CEO Gerry Smith of Office Depot, I placed my name on the audit committee so there would be input from a generalist. This position was especially needed regarding statement analysis, as the committee tended to be too legal and auditing heavy.

Below you will find the skills gap analysis which I completed by function, as well as by committee. In this example, I added the head of IT to the IT/Cyber committee with an advisor I recommended who was the former head of IT/Cyber for a major growth company. You can bring in board advisors for anything. I added an executive coach as a board advisor or director. Advisors may not have a vote, but they can dramatically shape the success of the business.

This company was hard and fast at a nine-member board with three executives, Sam, Bob, and Bill, along with six outside directors. The company also was set on keeping directors, so it made it challenging to meet all the needs of the company. The number of auditors and lawyers was overkill for the audit and compensation committee, but they likely wouldn't harm the business.

SUMMARY OF BOARD SKILLS REVIEW | Chart 10.1

Gaps ☒

Sam Townsend (Chairman & CEO)

AUDIT	COMP	Nom	CYBER/IT	EXECUTIVE COMMITTEE			
		Gov		Industry Relations	R&D OPS	Marketing Sustain	PEOPLE Dev.
Bob	Bob	☒	☒	Bill	Bill	Bill	Bill
Julie	Steve	☒	☒	☒	☒	☒	☒
Roberta	Julie				☒	☒	☒
Theresa							

Gaps Addressed

Sam Townsend (Chairman & CEO)

SPECIAL	AUDIT	COMP	Nom	CYBER/IT	EXECUTIVE COMMITTEE			
M&A			Gov		Industry Relations	R&D OPS	Marketing Sustain	PEOPLE Dev.
David	Bob	Bob	David	Scott	Bill	Bill	Bill	Bill
Johna	Julie	Steve	Scott	David	David	David	David	David
Sam	Roberta	Julie				Scott	Mark	Steph
	Theresa							
	David	David						

Summary of Board Skills Review

In this example, the company had two major divisions; one was an old-school food company, and the other was a fast-growing food technology firm that was licensing worldwide. The board committees are only what is necessary and stacked by audit professionals for audit and compensation. There was no nominating and governance committee. The company was going through the divestiture of a business so that they could internally fund acceleration in a growth area. Therefore, a special committee needed to be formed with experience in that area to handle the people, process, strategy, and sustainability of the organic business and help to direct further inorganic activity.

Sometimes when you present these gaps to management and a board, they will find other ways to cover them with advisors or management assistance, but it is a valuable exercise to flush out alignment.

I credit former Pepsi/Pizza Hut CEO Mike Lorelli, an outstanding NYU-Stern graduate, for his mentorship in the area of mediating board issues. He also recommended I become a part of the National Association of Corporate Directors (NACD) and the American College of Corporate Directors (ACCD), two excellent organizations that teach, mentor, and model for the industry as does the Association for Corporate Growth (ACG) with regard to middle market deal flow and growth. As Stephen Covey says, "sharpen the saw." Always look to improve your skills and ability. Focus on incremental improvement of your people, organization, company, management, and board.

Communication with Board Members, Advisors, and Investors

It is best to have transparent communication with your investors, board, and advisors regularly so they can stay informed and help guide the organization, especially in their area of specialty. The following list includes items that may need discussion and updates:

1. Metrics including revenue, units, number of customers, MOUs (Memorandums of Understanding), GKRs (from Strategic Planning chapter), KPIs (Key Performance Indices), online, and other channel reports should be reported. If you are acquiring business, the status of the inorganic pipeline is required.

2. Understand your cash position, your cash flow, and the quantification of your runway, which is the length of time you have before turning profitable or requiring additional funding. This is critical if you have to raise extra money in a venture situation or if you are close to production capacity and need to build additional

capacity to grow and handle the volume.

3. Report your product and service status. What is going well? What issues may be happening? What is the status of your pipeline research and development?

4. Be as specific as possible in reference to what you require relative to introductions, work performed, advice, and future funding initiatives.

5. Relay operational growth matters: numbers of employees, new hires, current and future openings, labor issues, and any matters that involve the press of the company or competition.

6. Use everyone's time wisely. Board members have the duty of loyalty. They are likely under confidentiality, but some investors and advisors may not be. So, be transparent, but use discretionary judgment because it is your duty to all the stakeholders to increase shareholder value. Most of all, efficiently utilize these resources.

Lesson Learned: Don't be afraid to get the best executive talent for your board and advisory board. The group can be tough, demanding, and challenging, but you are not going to incrementally improve sitting in a corn silo with a bunch of "yes" people. You have to hire extraordinary people to receive exceptional results.

SECTION 4

GIVING BACK

CHAPTER ELEVEN

PRINCIPLE XI: Understand the Importance of Giving Back with 1) Time & Talents, 2) Sharing Your Network of Contacts, & Direct Opportunities, & 3) Financial Resources.

Time and Talents

As a leader and team member, it's great to give back in a proactive, meaningful way to improve the world. It's one of my favorite things to do in life. To me, this is the greatest joy and is the best use of people, process, strategy, and sustainability. The principle of giving back is utilizing your time and talents, sharing your network of contacts and direct opportunities, and financial resources to make the world a better place.

You can by examining how you can contribute based on your skill set. Since this is giveback time, I am going to share with you some fun ways and causes through which I give back to the world. If you feel that you are not learning as much, the goal here is to get you to realize that anyone can give back. I have worked most of my life for six to seven days per week. I also raised my children and coached about a dozen football, softball, and baseball teams and pitched in at the rowing tent during regattas as well.

Tufts University Friedman School of Nutrition Science and Policy

The Tufts University Friedman School of Nutrition Science and Policy is in the top five of all nutrition programs in the world. I first learned about Tufts Nutrition School from President Jean Meyer when I was attending Tufts. It has grown into a world-class institution and is a leader in health, wellness, and nutrition. They are tackling the worldwide food crisis by utilizing the strength of innovation, research, and development. This work is a catalyst to bring government officials, nongovernmental agencies, profits, and nonprofits to solve and collaborate with a laser-sharp focus on health, wellness, sustainability, food, agriculture technology, restaurants, supplements, insurance, and to establish a physical ecosystem based out of Boston.

In the past few years, there has been a rapid increase in worldwide key stakeholders supporting time, treasure, and thoughts. I serve with

Dean Dary Mozaffarian, Academic Dean Edward Saltzman, Director Jeff Blumberg, staff, and the fine student body with innovation and entrepreneurship in this regard. I am humbled to be a part of it as an advisor, mentor, guest lecturer, and judge facilitator.

I send appreciation to my fellow advisors and supporting donors, council members in both profit and nonprofit, who are working to take on the worldwide food crisis. It takes a group to be able to finance, advise, and partner on these critical issues, and we are delighted with this impressive group of colleagues for stepping up with time and treasure to make it happen.

Changing the World One Smart Bowl at a Time

Dr. Robin Shrestha and Dr. Sapana Adhikari implemented their pitch and plan for a Smart Bakery in Manthali, Nepal. There is a massive problem of a worldwide food crisis of malnutrition and poverty. The team invented the Smart Bowl, which is a nutritious, vitamin-enriched bread bowl made in a mudbrick oven. The goal was to infuse nutrition to meet the needs of one village at a time with prospects that it would accelerate if the results were successful. They were the winners of the Nutrition Entrepreneurship Competition in 2018. Within a short time, it was a massive hit with the schoolchildren, selling out almost every day.

Tufts Food and Nutrition Entrepreneurship Competition

In 2019, Silvia Berciano Benitez and Nayla Bezares won the Tufts Food and Nutrition Entrepreneurship Competition with a great pitch and absolutely out of this world tasty oatmeal ice cream samples targeted to the Hispanic market. There was hope to test mainstream markets at a later time. This ice cream is fantastic and certainly healthier for you. It's a winner if they continue down that direction.

Photo 11.A
Picture of Dave facilitating the Nutrition competition judging in 2018.

For more information, please go to: https://nutrition.tufts.edu/entrepreneurship/competition

Website: www.nutrition.tufts.edu

Tufts Veterinary School

Tuffs veterinary school had a research project where I was called on to commercialize Anaconda Green-Blue Eggs. They needed a way to go to market. We were able to get the product placed with the Laflamme Family and Pete and Gerry's Eggs in New Hampshire. It successfully commercialized this unique niche market and turned a research project into a commercialized reality.

Tufts Gordon Institute: Graduate Innovation and Undergraduate Engineering and Entrepreneurship

Disrupting the Future

I've enjoyed working with the Tufts Gordon Institute in the Masters of Innovation Management Program with Dean Kevin Oye, the Tufts Entrepreneurship Center with Jack Derby, Tufts School of Engineering with Dean Chris Swan, as well as working with the Tufts all school $100K New Ventures Competitions with Professor Tina Weber. I met with teams several months prior to the competition to help them channel their thoughts and ideation into action. I then judged the semifinal round of a $100K competition.

Alex Rappaport and Zwitter

Alex Rappaport is currently the CEO of Zwitter. He has gone through initial seed funding, negotiated his IP, and has commercialized and is heading into an "A" round of funding with excellent prospects.

Peter "Peetee" Clay, a fraternity brother, and I judged the semifinals of the $100K Competition at Tufts University. Peetee was the original product manager on the Sensor razor for Gillette and later a senior executive there. Other judges wanted Alex, his team, and his proposed company Zwitter knocked out. Peetee and I looked at each other and saw there was something special about Alex beyond his presentation, which sorely needed improvement. We assisted Alex in getting to the finals. He worked diligently to reshape his pitch and the plan. He added a clear flowchart for the funding needed so that investors knew that they could fund each chain of success. He also sharpened every word to stimulate the croc brain and took the Innermetrix analysis so that he could understand his blind spots.

His team won his share of $100,000. In eighteen months, he raised $3.25 million including $1.25 million grant from the US Department of

Energy. federal grant for a sustainable initiative of removing pollutants from dirty water through a Tufts University IP technology. Alex puts cartel disruption principles into practice and I appreciate his passion to give back. The author is a proud limited partner of Zwitterco. I'm extraordinarily pleased with their success.

Website: www.zwitterco.com

Conrad Challenge: SAFE

In the spring of 2019, I had the opportunity to coach a team from Title I Nashua High School South in Nashua, New Hampshire. Could students as young as fourteen years old master the tools necessary to pitch and win the competition to start a business? I enjoyed coaching them with Kaitlin Gao. The students did their market research. They knocked the socks off of their pitch. The boys won an international competition held at the Kennedy Space Center headed by Nancy Conrad, the late astronaut Pete Conrad's widow.

The boys made it to the finals, and with their invention, they proved a principle for eliminating forest fires with metamaterials and low-frequency waves. The young men, including CEO Josh Gao and COO Sam Greenberg, pictured with Ady Shankar and Jeffrey Lam, won $240,000 in scholarships, along with computers, Pete Conrad sunglasses, and worldwide bragging rights! They received interest from the United States Navy, and they received introductions to new competitions, universities, and investors.

The boys studied at the summer Accelerator at Tufts Gordon Institute with Professor Tina Weber and support from Chairman Jack Derby, Dean Kevin Oye, and Dean Chris Swan. They also did some benchwork at the University of Massachusetts Lowell. Doug "Dougie" Kline, head of the IP Department of Goodwin Procter, a fellow DU Tufts alumnus, helped Josh, Sam, and the boys to get a provisional patent filed for the product.

At NASA, the boys killed the pitch. They had great graphical intrigue showing wildfires and had a well-practiced pitch that finished thirty seconds early. They had practiced answers to frequently asked questions and then ended their presentation with the advisor slide to bolster credibility for professionals backing them. The croc brain was neutralized in four minutes and thirty seconds! The neocortex backlash came when someone from the audience yelled out, "Take my card. I want to invest." Even the Navy officers that had been quite stoic during the competition cracked smiles. The president of Match.com was speechless, and the president of the Conrad Foundation said, "No one is in that space. Wow. You've really got something."

There were a few other entries that were quite impressive, but the group from Title I Nashua High School South won! The boys made such an impression that they were immediately invited with scholarships to go to the Nexus Summit in New York and to meet a slew of investors. Josh Gao, the CEO of the group, addressed the United Nations on behalf of the Conrad Challenge and SAFE.

If this pitching process can work for people as young as fourteen years old, as well as bring in hundreds of millions in financing in other situations that I have had participation… what can it do for you?

Photo 11.B

The SAFE boys with myself under the Saturn V Rocket next to Apollo Mission Control at the Kennedy Space Center in Florida, after winning the first place prize.

Website:

www.conradchallenge.org

www.safefire.tech

Tufts Legends of Innovation and Entrepreneurship:

Honoring the Very Best Disruptors, Accelerators, and Philanthropists

I have financed a bit and sweated with Jack Derby and Mark "Zig" Adzigian, of Tufts Development, to create the Tufts Legends of Innovation and Entrepreneurship Award and Speaker Series. Hundreds of people flooded a packed auditorium for the inaugural award. John Bello, the legendary innovator and founder of the soft drink company SoBe, NFL properties head and current chairman of Reed's and Boathouse Sports, won the award.

In Boston, steeped in sports tradition, there is good, better, and best. If you are good or better, "You suck" and need improvement. If you are the best, "You don't suck" and people smile. As legendary high school coach Bill Tighe used to say, "If I am not screaming at you, I don't care . . . and that's the worst." In Boston sports, Tom Brady, Bill Belichick, Bobby Orr, Larry

Bird, Bill Russell, Ted Williams, and David Ortiz don't suck. In innovation and entrepreneurship, John Bello does not suck. On top of his legendary success covered in the forward of this book, John has given back significantly in time, talents, and financial contributions. He continues to do so for Tufts University's athletic and innovation programs, along with guest lecturing. It is an honor to pay tribute to John's legendary success both in cartel disruption and for giving back. Tufts now gives Legends of Innovation and Entrepreneurship awards to deserving recipients in the spirit of giving back.

Photo 11.C

Here's a Picture from the inaugural Tufts Legends of Innovation and Entrepreneurship Award and Speaker Series in 2018 honoring John Bello. Pictured below are Athletic Director John Morris, yours truly, John Bello, and Jack Derby of the Tufts Entrepreneurship Center.

Constructive Diplomacy

When I was selling food to Cuba and working on potential life-saving technology back with the biotech group, I was able to engage in backdoor diplomacy between President Castro and certain senior high-ranking officials in Washington.

Service was requested because the official channels were at best caustic because of the lack of diplomatic relations due to the US embargo placed on Cuba. There was also the long-time family-based dispute that is best characterized as a hostile divorce battle for the island between the Communist regime and the US supported by Cuban Americans that included some leaders related to Fidel Castro.

Decades earlier, I worked for both the chief of staff, Andrew H. Card, at the White House, as well as the US Agency for International Development head, Andrew Natsios. At the time, I also was fortunate as New England Brown Egg Council president to have had some great relationships with several members of congress and senators.

Senior US officials needed confirmation that Cuba was open to third-party inspections of its biotech-related facilities. There was a charge by a senior state department official, John Bolton, that inferred the possibility of potential weapons of mass destruction following 9/11.

At the time, I was selling Castro agriculture goods. I had discussions with the biotech leadership on importing life-saving IP as well as perhaps later agriculture biotech IP. Further, I pitched in to help aid the safe return of US citizens that were being detained. The efforts were fruitful in getting them released.

Ironically, while doing business in Cuba, I used my downtime as an opportunity to have care packages sent to US soldiers in Iraq to one of US Army Colonel Robert McLaughlin's Units with Stephanie's assistance. Robert played next to me in High School as a center on our football offensive line. It seemed every time Robert got promoted, we had more packages to send. It was an honor and great privilege to send these soldiers a small token of our immense appreciation for their service and sacrifice. It was a precarious time, and life has a way of opening opportunities to help give service in many ways.

Nowadays, in 2020, Cuba is the number three market for poultry products. Cuba's trade with the US brings in hundreds of millions of dollars per year, which helps US farmers, distributors, and traders to secure necessary revenue for their families. In this situation, the US farmers, agribusiness, food, and medicine relationships with Cuba are a clear example of how constructive engagement and business relationships helped bridge common interests.

We also have helped many poor people with low-cost proteins and food in Cuba. Notwithstanding, I have friends and the most profound respect for the exile community living in Florida and New Jersey. I fully appreciate their position and their cause, which included raising questions they had directly with Castro at that time.

Photo 11.D
Pictured here in 2002, left to right, Pedro Alverez (president of the Cuban import company, Alimport), Cuban President Fidel Castro, Juanita Vera (interpreter), yours truly, and my Washington counsel, Phil Olsson.

Sharing Your Network of Contacts and Direct Opportunities

I started, along with the assistance of generations of graduates, the Fraternal Alumni Career Network in 1988 at the local Tufts chapter for a fraternity called Delta Upsilon (DU), which was a slightly different ecosystem than sports. Fraternities and sororities are changing with progressive times. As long as they behave themselves, they avail to opportunities, including a vast network.

We had a sports networking group that helped with the school as a whole. We wanted to give the students a niche network that would routinely help them with jobs, internships, and advice. I have assisted with the placement of hundreds of students into internships and employment. I've also been able to do this directly myself.

In 1993, I had an intern, Mike Frisoli, that received seventeen job offers after his internship for me. He took my advice and worked the network tirelessly. Mike has become tremendously successful as a real estate brokerage executive in Boston and is now a managing director with fellow fraternity brother and athlete J. R. McDonald. They have given back significantly to Tufts.

My intern at the time, Matt Keller, had the opportunity to meet with Fidel Castro's foreign ministry. He was able to network with top players in food and agriculture in Cuba. He also attended the famous Snow Bowl football game between the New England Patriots and Oakland Raiders, where he connected with his next position courtesy of a fellow fraternity member and fellow athlete Kevin Cloherty and Bob Tishman. I bring this to light because it's crucial to network and develop a network. Your network is a great asset.

What Can You Do?

Giving back doesn't have to be related to sports, fraternities, sororities, or your school's alumni council. Consider contributing to religious organizations, social clubs, professional organizations, friends, family, and networking organizations. People like to hire and spend time with individuals that will positively influence their life.

I was out to dinner last year with a group of professional women that said men do a better job at networking than women. Just for the record, the greatest networker that I know is my daughter Jess, and she doesn't realize she's networking. She's part of the rowing world as a rower, coach, and official. I have never seen such a vast, mutually supportive network that has worldwide reach to network with men and women.

Whenever she travels, she has people that she knows or people that are friends of friends that share something meaningful in common.

They all are a passionate, motivated, and successful group from different socioeconomic backgrounds. You don't need to be an Olympic or college athlete to be a part of it, just the willingness and desire to learn and practice.

Photo 11.E

At the Head of the Charles Regatta for Community Rowing Inc (CRI), Boston, MA

The best networker that I know doesn't realize she's a networker. This picture is of my daughter Jess with her team.

Financial Resource Support

At Radlo Foods, we chose to give 10 to 33 percent of our profit to invest in important causes. We also created some disruption along the way. I'm going to share with you a few of the interesting causes.

Team Impact: A Compassionate Solution to a Societal Problem

Jay Calnan and Danny Kraft have been a shining example of giving back to repair the world through philanthropy. They set up a charity that placed children with life-threatening illnesses on college sports teams. The children are drafted to become full members of the team. When they had chemotherapy or surgery, the young adults on the team would send text messages and give other methods of support to the children and their families. The team was there to support the family.

Jay called me at the beginning of this project and said, "I need your help to start this off." My answer was clear, "How much, and when?" I had dinner at one of the first annual fundraisers with coach Bill Belichick, who was kind enough to support the charity.

Many others purchased tickets and tables to the inaugural event. Fellow fraternity brothers and athletes like Daniel "Dots" Doherty, Rob "Tish" Tishman, Joe "Joey" Klein, Doug Kline, Doug Colton, and Mark Madigan, as well others in the greater community, like Chris Kenney, supported the event. Tufts athletes and coaches such as Jay Civetti, John Casey, and the athletic director, John Morris, have been great supporters of this venture. From the Boston test market program, it has accelerated into several offices and to colleges and teams from coast to coast. The annual fundraiser gala hosted by Wendi Nix of ESPN draws tremendous support and raises now millions of dollars every year for this outstanding cause.

Team IMPACT has achieved its primary mission to provide this service to every single kid and family in America that needs this type of support. It's been a fantastic ride. It took great leadership, strategy, people, process, and an outstanding value proposition to make it happen!

Website: www.goteamimpact.org

Concussion Legacy Foundation: Tackling a Major Headache while Disrupting Cartels

Chris Nowinski of the Concussion Legacy Foundation highlighted a significant crisis. He disrupted many sports business cartels worldwide to change concussion protocols and treatment. This disruption extended to the suppliers and support apparatus with research and awareness of the dangers of concussions relative to chronic traumatic encephalopathy (CTE). CTE is a neurodegenerative disease caused by repeated head injuries.

When we were kids, I didn't understand why I did well academically, but on timed college boards, I was unable to perform adequately. I later realized it was the concussions I had sustained playing under the old school athletic system of, "If you can see two fingers after you sustained an injury, go back in and finish playing." We have come a long way in just a few decades.

My daughter Jess had seven concussions from rowing in high school, club, and college. We were concerned that she could get CTE and concerned about her rehabilitation. After a cold call to Chris, he was able to assure us based upon his latest research that she was not at risk for CTE because her accidents were freak, like getting a boat dropped on her or a paddle to the head. He said that CTE comes from sub-concussive hits sustained over years of playing contact sports. This situation was especially true at young ages, such as with Pop Warner, the largest and oldest youth football in the world. He also was able to refer us to the best long-term therapists who are a leader in the NFL concussion protocol program to help Jess repair and recover from her injury long-term.

The above is an important story, as it gave me a pathway to learn about concussions, CTE, and other brain-related issues. Many people get caught up in the fight to maintain and increase safety in sports. They fail to recognize the vast areas of how Chris Nowinski and the Concussion Legacy Foundation have dramatically improved athletes, firefighters, active and retired military, and others to incrementally progress their lives in a powerful and meaningful way.

Jess and I support Chris and Dr. Robert Cantu and their excellent work in bringing these critical issues and research to light. In their next frontier, they are expanding their research for military veterans to deal with mental disorders, along with growing their brain banks of study worldwide. The research is important work that deserves our support as they tackle this global problem and continue to fight cartels at home and abroad. Keep it up Chris and Robert!

Website: www.concussionfoundation.org

The Finca Vigía Foundation (formerly known as the Hemingway Preservation Foundation): Incubating by Building a Bridge over Troubled Waters through Common Agreement of Appreciation of a Literary Hero

While doing business in Cuba in the 2000s, I gave early seed financial support to Frank Phillips, a respected journalist with the *Boston Globe*, his late wife Jenny, and Mary-Jo Adams, executive director of the Hemingway Preservation Foundation. Bob Vila, American home improvement television show host, later joined the foundation as co-president. We worked on a combined US and Cuba project to restore Ernest Hemingway's home, boat, and artifacts in Cuba. When countries and people are at war or in a cold war, sometimes you need to start by agreeing to something of common interest.

Seed capital was needed to get the project off the ground, and later, the foundation was able to get crucial corporate funding. If you visit the home on the outskirts of Havana, you will see Hemingway's boat, writing area, and you will see my Uncle Andre Kostelanetz's record playing on Mr. Hemingway's record player. Hemingway was a big fan of Uncle Andre's music. I was delighted to support this project. Ernest and the foundation were kind enough to pay tribute to Uncle Andre.

Website: www.fincafoundation.org

Cuba-US Interests: Incubating Friendship, Good Will, and Capitalism

As a portion of our profitable sales to Cuba, Radio Foods supported the US Interests Section (embassy building) for their holiday display. It included Frosty the Snowman and holiday decorations, which was pitched by Ambassador Cason, the kind Susan Archer, and tougher than nails Usha Pitts. The display lit up the Havana night skyline as well as the Malecon road and walkway between the US Embassy and the ocean. It has continued to do so for decades. I never thought that Frosty the Snowman and the decorations would end up in an international diplomatic war between the US and Cuba over other issues, but creative diplomats found a way.

Fortunately, our US industry's business relationship with Cuba has been strong enough to withstand the political back and forth. I had a two-hour discussion with Fidel Castro that focused on Harrington, Locke, and the founders' philosophy. This situation was one of the few times being a political philosophy major in college aided my efforts.

I quoted Harrington, who said, "Politics flows from economics." We had a substantial opportunity to grow business, and we did. Castro countered, "David, mira, en Cuba, politicos de economicos, o economicos de politicos, decide Daveed." Castro usually did not speak English. Translated, this means, "Listen, in Cuba, politics comes from economics or economics comes from politics. I'll let you decide, David." The customers are always right, especially Latin American dictators that pay cash up front. The Cubans never held Frosty and the Christmas display against me, my company, or the industry. The industry has gone from zero business to billions, with blockbuster growth!

I am pictured below with Cason, who was a rabble-rousing head of the US Interests Section (ambassador). Jim and I are still friends. He's a bright and creative guy that later became mayor of Coral Gables, Florida, after his State Department years. At the time, we agreed to disagree on certain policies. However, we shared the love of the US Embassy residence in Cuba both inside and outside, with the gardens where Jim grew US-Cuban tobacco along with organic fruits and vegetables. The residence itself has a great history, and I encourage you to read Jim Cason's book about it. Also pictured here is Howard Helmer of the American Egg Board. He was the World Omelet Champion in the Guinness Book of World Records.

Photo 11.F

Summary

Giving back in time, contacts, and resources is where leveraging people, process, strategy, and sustainability matters. Time, contacts, and treasure are crucial to support and repair the world. You don't have to dish out millions to be of service. You have skills that people need. I work with executives, professionals, workers, students, parents, young adults, and children. There are many areas where you can make a difference. Get in the game! Help disrupt major problems with solutions that matter.

Afterword

What's hot on Dave's new trend list? Here's the latest on the trend list from the social-healthy, technological, sustainable economic, and environmental factors.

Christine McCracken, a protein analyst from Rabobank, delivered a speech to the USA Poultry and Egg Export Council (USAPEEC) in Washington, DC, on December 11, 2019. She said emerging consumer trends are disrupting the protein market with healthy, sustainable, and animal welfare factors. It plays well for certain animal-based products like poultry, based on sustainable feed conversion, a low carbon footprint, and it's on-trend with health.

However, the push with plant-based protein initiatives is showing some strong promise in those segments. According to a *Refrigerated & Frozen Foods* article on December 11, 2019, data shows 31 percent YOY CAGR projected through 2025 for plant-based meats. Animal meat has been growing at .9 percent CAGR. This category as a whole does not take into account value-added healthy products that are growing faster, and the number of animal-based products is a much broader base. Plant-based burgers are increasing at a 20 percent YOY CAGR rate now in Europe and at 8 percent in the United States. The evidence is based on the UBS Evidence Lab in New York that surveyed over three thousand consumers, fifty restaurant franchisees, and reviewed over twenty million social media interactions. They also interviewed over twenty protein scientists and supply chain experts.

These impressive growth statistics are due to animal activist innovators and accelerators looking for better food for their vegan community in addition to growth into mainstream segments. This plant-based "clean meat" movement came at the tail end of taking on the industry over Cage Free and Humane Welfare campaigns. The campaigns were driven by the Humane Society of the United States (HSUS), which included Josh Balk, Paul Shapiro, Wayne Pacelle, Mike Markarian, and Miyun Park. This revolution is primarily based upon social drivers, but the big financiers are looking for mainstream growth in the protein sector.

Will Sawyer, the lead economist of CoBank, noted at the USAPEEC Conference that there is strong growth in agriculture and food technology. It's driving out costs in labor and increasing efficiency in the supply chain. Separately, there has also been some outstanding hydroponic technology introduced that reduces water intake drastically, decreases the land required, and eliminates diseases that occur in the soil. Food technology, agriculture technology, and innovative technology are sprouting up like weeds to address the decline of water and acceptable land for farming.

Words of Wisdom from the Late, Great Jim Valvano: Former North Carolina State Championship Basketball Coach

The innovation business isn't easy. It can be quite challenging at times. I wanted to share some insight with you from the courageous championship basketball coach, Jim Valvano, who fought and eventually succumbed to a life-threatening disease.

"To me, there are three things we all should do every day. We should do this every day of our lives. Number one is to laugh. You should laugh every day. Number two is to think. You should spend some time in thought. And number three is you should have your emotions moved to tears, could be happiness or joy. But think about it. If you laugh, you think, and you cry, that's a full day. That's a heck of a day. You do that seven days a week . . . you're going to have something special."

ESPY AWARDS, 1993

Notes

1. Klaff, Oren. *Pitch Anything: An Innovative Method for Presenting, Persuading, and Winning the Deal*. New York: McGraw-Hill, 2011, 12.

2. Klaff, Oren. *Pitch Anything*, p. 17.

3. Klaff, Oren. *Pitch Anything*, p. 125.

4. Klaff, Oren. *Pitch Anything*, p. 127.

5. Kittaneh, Firas. "10 Ways Competition Can Improve Your Business." *Entrepreneur*, August 17, 2015. https://www.entrepreneur.com/article/249541.

6. "Competitive Analysis." *Entrepreneur*, August 1, 2006. https://www.entrepreneur.com/article/25756.

7. Ingram, David. "The Advantages of Competitive Analysis in Strategic Planning." *Chron*, November 21, 2017. https://smallbusiness.chron.com/advantages-competitive-analysis-strategic-planning-18331.html.

8. Mathews, Devin. "The 7 Deadly Sins of Private Equity." *Business Insider*, September 21, 2016. https://www.businessinsider.com/the-deadly-sins-of-private-equity-2016-9.

About the Author:

David Radlo is an accomplished CEO, outside director, and trusted advisor. His accomplishments in his twenty-eight years as a CEO include delivering a six-fold EBITDA increase and a thirty-fold increase in enterprise value. Radlo has an uncanny ability to find a path to a profitable sea change in the growth CAGR and the ability to envision synergistic partnerships, alliances, and organic and inorganic targeted growth initiatives.

He is presently a partner with RB Markets-Achievemost and is a CEO, board member, advisor, and partner to biotech, agriculture, consumer, and technology business. He has worked on $1.7 billion in acquisitions. Experienced in the US and globally (personally negotiated an agreement with Fidel Castro), Radlo is working with private equity firms, private companies, family businesses, and venture firms. He is a Board Governance Fellow of NACD, Professional Outside Director (ACCD), and Trusted Advisor and guest lecturer of the Tufts University Friedman School of Nutrition Science and Policy. He's also a mentor, guest lecturer, and certified coach of the Tufts University Entrepreneurship Center, Graduate Innovation Program, and Engineering School.

After a rewarding educational experience and member of the football program at Tufts University as a player, Radlo later became a recruiter while coaching elsewhere. He bridged his experiential learning at Tufts with a five-year career in public service, political advocacy, and working with the US Congress and Massachusetts General Court. He subsequently ran a strong race for state representative, receiving 39 percent of the votes, commencing as a senior in college. He worked for H. W. Bush on the 1988 campaign, turned down potential opportunities at the White House and State Department, and finally turned to the traditional business sector. He accepted a management position with Citibank to spearhead the marketing and sales for their equivalent of Western Union. He left Citibank to enter NYU-Stern for his MBA and later worked for Chase.

Radlo took a management role in a generational family business and later founded Radlo Foods, a company entrenched in brown, specialty, domestic, and international commodity eggs, wholesale food distribution, specialty foods, and a partnership in biotech with Vicam. At Vicam, they advanced food safety and partnered with scientists from MIT, Harvard, BU, and Johns Hopkins.

Fast-forward a decade, and the biotech company was sold to a strategic partner at high enterprise value. At Radlo Foods, Radlo expanded operations to thirty states and reached out to EMEA, Canada, the Caribbean, and Asia Pacific. The company footprinted and replicated specialty designer eggs and products that exploded the category through segmentation, creation of two national brands, and several private label brands that led to YOY double-digit growth. Also, he was adept at fostering appropriate add-on acquisitions. He then sold to Land O'Lakes for substantial enterprise value.

Radlo has served on all committees of the American Egg Board, as well as the USA Poultry and Egg Export Council, where he helped shape the US trade policy. He was also president of the New England Brown Egg Council. His board and advisory experience include Next Remedies Cannabis, Parkinson's Biotechnology, Charlesbank Capital Partners, Blockchain Made Easy, Radlo Foods (Egg-Land's Best and Born Free), Vicam Biotech, and H&M Entertainment Ventures. His nonprofit board and advisory include Tufts University Friedman School of Nutrition Science and Policy and other Tufts-related Innovation programs, athletics, and fraternal, as well as support for several charities. He is an active member of the National Association of Corporate Directors (NACD), the American College of Corporate Directors (ACCD), and Association for Corporate Growth (ACG). Radlo has been a guest lecturer at Tufts University and NYU Stern School of Business.

In addition to degrees from Tufts and NYU, he received an honorary degree from Boston College. Radlo is a certified management consultant, interim CEO, trusted advisor, and executive coach. He has a US patent pending and twenty-one trademarks assigned. He resides in the Boston area, where he enjoys watching his kids develop their sports skills and develop intellectually and emotionally. He's also watching them develop their business, management, and communication skills. Then, with whatever time and weather is left . . . he gets in some rounds of golf.

To Contact David Radlo's office: info@achievemost.com

CPSIA information can be obtained
at www.ICGtesting.com
Printed in the USA
BVHW080219061121
620875BV00003B/14